U.S. Joint Forces Command
JOINT WARFIGHTING CENTER
116 LAKE VIEW PARKWAY
SUFFOLK, VA 23435 2697

MESSAGE TO THE JOINT WARFIGHTERS

As US Joint Forces Command continues to interact with the combatant commands and Services, we recognize that there is very little doctrinal guidance on integrating financial operations. Consequently, we have developed this pre-doctrinal handbook to help joint force commanders and their staffs understand the scope and importance of integrated financial operations and provide information and guidance on its process; best practices; planning, execution, and assessment considerations; and resources.

Integrated financial operations are the integration, synchronization, prioritization, and targeting of fiscal resources and capabilities along with the related efforts of interagency and multinational partners and nongovernmental organizations against an enemy, and in support of the population, combined with minimizing the possibility that such resources/capabilities will be diverted or inadvertently misused to support an enemy's financial networks. Further, integrated financial operations encompasses more than simple fiscal policy and oversight—they entail using finances to support operational objectives. Accordingly, the joint force commander requires the ability to manage limited financial resources within the Department of Defense and coordinate with other US Government and host nation agencies, multinational forces, intergovernmental organizations, and nongovernmental organizations to fully utilize financial resources in the accomplishment of operational objectives.

As the *Capstone Concept for Joint Operations* contends, US forces should "focus on operational objectives whose achievement suggests the broadest and most enduring results."[1] Therefore, every joint force commander should provide guidance for the planning, execution, and assessment of integrated financial operations that seek to refine the associated processes and procedures among military and non-military organizations.

During the recent past, our understanding of integrated financial operations and its impact on joint operations has continued to evolve, particularly from our experiences in Afghanistan. These experiences and insights are described in this handbook. I encourage you to use the information in this handbook and provide feedback to help us capture value-added ideas for incorporation in emerging joint doctrine.

JOSEPH REYNES, JR.
Major General, USAF
Director, Joint Concept Development &
Experimentation (J9)

STEPHEN R. LAYFIELD
Major General, U. S. Army
Director, J7/Joint Warfighting Center

PREFACE

1. Scope

This handbook provides an understanding of the emerging processes and procedures being employed by joint force commanders (JFCs) and their staffs in planning, executing, and assessing efforts to integrate financial operations into their joint operation/campaign plans. It provides fundamental principles, techniques, and considerations related to integrated financial operations (IFO) that are being employed in the field and are evolving toward incorporation into joint doctrine publications.

2. Purpose

This handbook provides users with a pre-doctrinal reference describing how to employ IFO principles to achieve operational objectives. Its primary purpose is to improve the US military's use of financial operations through educating the user on joint IFO basics, best practices, and processes.

3. Background and Content

a. Although not without historical precedent, the idea of IFO has emerged from the experiences gained during US military operations in Iraq and Afghanistan. The impetus for this handbook originated with a request from US Forces – Afghanistan. As a result, the research and the examples used throughout this handbook will draw primarily from experiences in Afghanistan, but will propose solutions that will be of value to the JFC in any operational area.

b. IFO has two major aspects: 1) funding of economic development and infrastructure projects to win the support of a local population and to separate that population from an insurgency and, 2) contribute to destroying the insurgents' financial networks. More than a purely military effort, IFO seeks to refine processes and procedures that improve the synchronization and prioritization efforts among the USG agencies, multinational forces, IGOs, and NGOs.

c. Specifically, this handbook provides:

(1) Fundamental background information on IFO, its objectives, and required capabilities;

(2) Considerations for developing visibility of planned and ongoing related activities and coordination with potentially numerous, non-military stakeholders;

(3) A description of the essential elements of counter threat finance (CTF) and how these can be integrated into the IFO process;

(4) A discussion of specific training requirements for effective planning, execution, and assessment of IFO; and

(5) A compilation of current best practices that also may serve as a bridge between current practices in the field and their migration into doctrine.

4. Development

IFO, as a means to attain operational objectives, is not currently addressed in joint doctrine. United States Joint Forces Command (USJFCOM) developed this handbook to codify, at the operational level, practices emerging to fill this existing shortfall. Extensive research into organizations, processes, policies, and regulations that govern the execution of financial operations is the foundation of this handbook. More importantly, development included close coordination with, and significant input from, both civilian and military experts. The content was regularly vetted with these experts to assure relevance and accuracy of both theory and practice. As a result, this handbook represents the current state of best practices and offers recommended solutions to improve the JFC's ability to conduct IFO.

5. Application

This handbook is designed to provide the joint community with essential information on the rationale for IFO use, principles for using IFO, and lessons learned from how this concept has been employed in past and ongoing operations. Although this handbook contains extracts from some doctrinal and pre-doctrinal publications, it is not approved joint doctrine. Rather, it is a non-authoritative supplement to the current, extremely limited, documentation on the military use of funding for economic development and stabilization projects to achieve operational objectives. It offers some useful techniques, processes, and procedures that can be used in the combatant commands by JFCs and their staffs. More importantly, it acknowledges the role, resources, and implications for achieving operational objectives in the presence of the multiple agencies and organizations involved in financial operations that are beyond the formal command and control of military commanders.

6. Contact Information

Comments and suggestions on this important topic are welcome. The USJFCOM Joint Concept Development and Experimentation Directorate points of contact (POCs) are Lieutenant Colonel Ed Keller, USAF, at 757-203-3417 and e-mail: donald.keller@jfcom.mil; Mr. Ronald Rosenkranz, at 757-203-3348 and e-mail: ronald.rosenkranz@jfcom.mil; and Mr. Thomas Baldwin, at 757-686-9852 and e-mail: thomas.baldwin@saic.com. The USJFCOM J7/Joint Warfighting Center, Doctrine and Education Group, POCs are Lieutenant Colonel Jeffrey Martin, USAF, at 757-203-6871 and email: jeffrey.martin@jfcom.mil; and Mr. Chuck Shaver at 757-203-6062 and email: charles.shaver.ctr@jfcom.mil.

TABLE OF CONTENTS

CHAPTER V
OPERATIONAL IMPLICATIONS

- **Complements and supplements (rather than supplants) extant joint doctrine for planning, execution, and assessment of financial operations at the operational level**

- **Describes the elements of integrated financial operations (IFO) including the capabilities required for implementation**

- **Introduces planning considerations for incorporation of IFO into joint operation/campaign planning**

- **Identifies key stakeholders and potential partners in implementing IFO, recognizing the need for an inclusive, holistic approach**

- **Addresses assessment and the joint implications of conducting IFO**

- **Identifies the training requirements for implementation of IFO**

- **Provides recommendations and identifies best practices as a baseline for further development and refinement of IFO**

- **Discusses the operational implications of IFO**

Scope and Purpose

The Commander's Guide to Integrated Financial Operations (IFO) has two major aspects: 1) funding of economic development projects to win the support of a local population and to separate them from the insurgency; and, 2) contributing to destroying the insurgents' financial networks. More than fiscal policy, financial assistance, and accounting oversight, IFO seeks to refine processes and procedures to synchronize efforts among the United States Government (USG) agencies, multinational forces, intergovernmental organizations (IGOs), and nongovernmental organizations (NGOs). The continuing military problem that this commander's guide seeks to mitigate is the JFC's inability to integrate, synchronize, prioritize, and target the application of financial resources with the complementary efforts of USG agencies, multinational forces, IGOs, and NGOs to separate populations from insurgents and destroy or disrupt insurgent financial networks. As a means of mitigating the adverse effects of the identified shortfalls, it introduces changes needed to plan and execute IFO. To this end, the guide describes a process and organizational solution that could provide the JFC with the ability to use financial operations as an integral part of attaining joint operation/campaign objectives.

Overview

IFO can contribute directly to national and operational objectives. The overall principles and objectives of IFO have a much wider application and extend beyond traditional military boundaries. **Effective employment of IFO requires a holistic approach and an understanding of the roles, resources, and implications of the multiple agencies and organizations beyond the control of military commanders.** To conduct IFO, the JFC must leverage money and contracting assets that contribute to joint operation/campaign objectives; constructively engage non-military organizations in operational area; and identify valid, reliable, and achievable indicators and benchmarks. This requires awareness of past, ongoing, and planned projects; fully trained and capable personnel; and, common metrics and a process or guidelines that enable effective assessment. Shortfalls in the ability to achieve these requirements include, but are not limited to insufficient ability to obtain and maintain situational awareness and transparency of ongoing financial operations; inadequate ability to understand the multiple funding sources and complex processes; and, inability to provide oversight and monitoring of ongoing stabilization or development projects.

Planning Considerations

To coordinate and leverage efforts in the operational area effectively, the JFC and their staffs need to integrate financial operations fully into the joint operation planning process (JOPP). IFO calls for visibility and coordination of the multiple ongoing stability and development efforts and the organizations undertaking them in the JFC's assigned operational area. Coordinating and integrating efforts between the JFC and USG and host nation (HN) agencies, multinational forces, IGOs, and NGOs cannot be equated to the command and control (C2) of a military operation. Coordination among all the organizations involved in financial operations will increase integration resulting in greater synchronization and prioritization.

JFCs must possess the knowledge and ability to know at any given time, the different efforts (developmental and stabilizing) that are being proposed or initiated, the status of these efforts, personnel/organizations involved with those efforts, important contact points, their end results, and any important warnings regarding suspected corrupt entities or personnel. Counter threat financing (CTF) can contribute to IFO by eliminating not only insurgent funding, but also identifying host government corruption.

The Civil-Military Operations Center (CMOC), currently recognized in joint doctrine, emerges as the most appropriate structure for the planning, coordination, execution, and assessment of IFO. The CMOC is a mechanism that can serve as the primary coordination interface for operational- and tactical-level coordination between the JFC and other stakeholders. A CMOC may include representatives of US and multinational forces, USG and HN agencies, IGOs, NGOs, and the private sector. A framework for structured civil-military interaction, such as a CMOC, allows the military and non-military organizations to meet and work together in advancing common goals. Issues related to creating an IFO capability within a joint force include, but are not limited to, specific roles and responsibilities, composition, authorities, and knowledge management requirements.

Conducting the interorganizational coordination required for IFO requires a departure from traditional military thinking. The legacy requirement for C2 is not appropriate for operational structures and environments where the military commander does not possess clear authority over all activities of interest in his operational area. At various times, the JFC draws on the capabilities of other USG organizations or provides capabilities to or merely de-conflicts his activities with non-military organizations.

Assessing the Impact of Conducting Integrated Financial Operations

Accurate assessment and usable measures of effectiveness (MOE), as well as trained staff, are vital to successfully IFO. In order to identify and collect the proper data to support assessment; clear and concise objectives, outputs, and the impact for the proposed activity need to be defined to ensure success and proper measurement. In COIN and stability operations, accurately gauging the effect of money is dependent upon the ability of the JFC to measure the effectiveness or impact of development projects on the local population. There are many different assessment tools available and their use depends on the type of projects being conducted and the environment in which the projects are being implemented. An assessment tool is only as valid as the methodology used and robust training is needed to insure assessments are conducted properly.

Training Requirements

Training is necessary to ensure proper implementation of IFO. Although Department of Defense (DOD) policy mandates effective and timely training; frequently, personnel engaged in financial operations are not adequately trained prior to deployment. Lack of trained staff is not a result of inadequate training materials available, but more due to a lack of knowledge concerning what required training is available and when. Currently, in order to meet the strategic requirements of IFO, the JFCs and their staffs must combine tactical financial operations training with doctrine on joint operations, specifically taking note of the interorganizational environment. By ensuring the joint force staff possesses adequate knowledge and training in these areas, the JFC will be able to effectively integrate financial operations into the overall joint operation/campaign plan.

Operational Implications

More work needs to be done to identify an end state for IFO within DOD, analyze existing doctrinal processes to determine needed modification, and provide organizational constructs to support the process changes. Investigating and implementing ways to reach out and coordinate IFO activities with interagency, multinational, and other partners will provide significantly improved coherence and unity of effort towards achieving the joint operation/ campaign objectives. Full and effective implementation requires adopting doctrine, organization, training, materiel, leadership and education, personnel, and facilities (DOTMLPF) solutions. For example, to better facilitate implementation of IFO, the joint community needs to incorporate the IFO process, as described in Chapter II of this handbook, into joint doctrine. This effort should include defining the scope and limitations of IFO, identifying value-added organizational change and practices, and supporting capabilities and relationships. Continuing implementation and evaluation of IFO should consider the consequences across the DOTMLPF spectrum.

Summary

IFO are a necessary and critical capability in support of COIN and stability operations. IFO should be fully integrated into all operations processes at the outset and synchronized throughout planning, preparation, execution, and assessment to ensure the greatest contribution to the achievement of joint operation/campaign objectives. Effectively employed IFO can potentially achieve national and operational – level objectives that may pre-empt the requirement for combat operations.

CHAPTER I
OVERVIEW

1. Introduction

> *"In the five-year struggle to finish the war in Iraq, military leaders and their troops have said a particular weapon is among the most effective in their arsenal—American cash."*
>
> **"Money as a Weapon," Washington Post, 11 August 2008**

a. Recent and ongoing operations in Iraq and Afghanistan have demonstrated the value of employing a combination of lethal and nonlethal actions to achieve operational objectives. Among the latter is the directed use of finances to support the local population and to simultaneously combat the insurgencies. The concept of directed use of finances most recently emerged under the sobriquet of "Money as a Weapon System" (MAAWS) and has been adopted by some senior US military commanders whose guidance for counterinsurgency (COIN) operations includes "employing MAAWS emphasizing the need to maximize the throw weight of each round expended, or in this case, dollar spent." Specifically, this means ensuring the monies of each engagement contributed to the units' overall objectives.[2]

b. The use of MAAWS is evolving into a concept for integrated financial operations (IFO).[3] This name change from MAAWS recognizes that IFO is not solely a military issue; one of the primary complicating factors in execution of IFO is the number of diverse organizations potentially engaged in or affected by IFO employment. These organizations include multiple elements of the United States Government (USG), multinational partners, intergovernmental organizations (IGOs), and nongovernmental organizations (NGOs)—a complex mix of stakeholders, assets, expertise, and mission objectives.

c. IFO can contribute directly to the national and operational objectives. Militarily, IFO can be considered a capability to support irregular warfare (IW)—a violent struggle among state and non-state actors for legitimacy and influence over the relevant population(s). IW favors a full range of military and non-military approaches, often applied indirectly and asymmetrically to erode an adversary's power, influence, and will. The overall principles and objectives of IFO, however, have a much wider application and extend beyond traditional military boundaries. As promulgated in Department of Defense Instruction (DODI) 3000.05, *Stability Operations*, "[DOD] shall assist other USG agencies, foreign governments and security forces, and international governmental organizations in planning and executing reconstruction and stabilization efforts, to include...fostering economic stability and development". In order to assist economic recovery, the IFO concept emerged to guide military forces in the use of financial resources, with respect to the multiple stakeholders that may be involved in any one theater, and coordinate financial assets to meet a common objective.

d. Simply stated, IFO is the coordinated use of finances, goods, or services to support operational objectives. It has two major aspects: 1) funding of economic development projects to win the support of a local population and to separate them from the insurgency and, 2) contributing to destroying the insurgents' financial networks. IFO is more than fiscal policy, financial assistance, and accounting oversight. It seeks to refine processes and procedures to synchronize efforts among USG agencies, multinational partners, IGOs, and NGOs. Joint publication (JP) 1, *Doctrine for the Armed Forces of the United States*, contends: "The ability of the United States to achieve its national strategic objectives is dependent on the effectiveness of the USG in employing the instruments of national power. The appropriate governmental officials, often with National Security Council direction, normally coordinate these instruments of national power (diplomatic, informational, military, and economic)."

e. Recognizing both the potential to contribute to the warfighter's toolset, and the lack of joint doctrine in this emerging area, US Joint Forces Command (USJFCOM) directed development of this handbook.

2. Purpose: Why This Handbook is Necessary

"The shortfalls on the reconstruction side stem, to a significant degree, from the lack of a system within the US government for managing contingency relief and reconstruction operations. The lack of a good management framework meant that there were ineffective lines of authority and accountability among and between military and civilian organizations. This led to a lack of unity of command and weakened the program's unity of effort."

Stuart W. Bowen, Jr., Inspector General Office of the Special Inspector General for Iraq Reconstruction, March 25, 2009

a. This handbook project originated in response to a request from US Forces Afghanistan (USFOR-A) to USJFCOM requesting assistance to develop an IFO concept.[4] Initial attempts to employ the principles of IFO have been challenging. The continuing military problem, that this handbook seeks to mitigate, is the joint force commander's (JFC's) inability to integrate, synchronize, prioritize, and target the application of fiscal resources with the related efforts of interagency and multinational partners, IGOs, and NGOs in order to separate populations from insurgents and destroy or disrupt insurgent financial networks. Handbooks currently in use primarily provide tactical direction to deploying forces rather than operational or strategic analysis and solutions. Further, none of these adequately address counter threat finance (CTF) activities designed to deny, disrupt, destroy, or defeat financial systems and networks that negatively affect US interests.[5]

b. Effective employment of IFO requires unified action, i.e., the synchronization, coordination, and/or integration of the activities of governmental and nongovernmental entities with military operations to achieve unity of effort. The need for an integrated effort in Afghanistan was recognized after several years of ad hoc activities prompted by the US Civilian-Military Campaign Plan. The US Civilian-Military Campaign Plan calls for better integration of reconstruction projects, not only between US agencies but also with the international donor community. In current and future areas of operation, multiple USG and other organizations will be involved in similar activities. For example, the United States Agency for International Development (USAID) is the primary USG provider of humanitarian and economic assistance, a mission that mandates coordination between USAID and military commands responsible for operating in the same area. Therefore, this handbook acknowledges the roles, resources, implications, and authorities of the multiple agencies and organizations are beyond the control of JFCs. The handbook contains brief descriptions of the organizations most likely to be involved in development activities and provides some "best practices" to the JFC for effectively dealing with them. The handbook offers useful techniques, processes, and procedures that can be used in the combatant commands by JFCs and their staffs. It discusses the requirements of IFO and existing capabilities that can meet those requirements. The handbook provides the needed joint context and extrapolates the lessons derived in one operational area (Afghanistan) for global application.

KEY TERMS

Integration - The arrangement of military forces and their actions to create a force that operates by engaging as a whole.

Synchronization - The arrangement of military actions in time, space, and purpose to produce maximum relative combat power at a decisive place and time

Targeting - The process of selecting and prioritizing targets and matching the appropriate response to them, considering operational requirements and capabilities.

JP 1-02, Department of Defense Dictionary of Military and Associated Terms

Prioritization - To list or rate (as projects or goals) in order of priority.

© *2010 Merriam-Webster*

---

3. The Elements of Integrated Financial Operations

a. Since no formal concept for IFO exists, a process model of IFO was developed, evaluated, and vetted by a community of interest (COI) that included USG, IGO, and NGO experts. The intent was to determine the process and high-level requirements for effective utilization of IFO.[6] **The resultant IFO process model consists of six interrelated steps** described individually below.

(1) **Evaluation of requirement validity and anticipated benefits:** To determine if the project is a bona fide mission need and the degree to which it will contribute to the overall operational objectives, its impact on other regional efforts, and its sustainability.

(2) **Determination of a source of funding**: Identification of the resources available and appropriate to support the project.

(3) **Validation of the project requirement**: Recommendation to the person with the authority and ability to direct execution.

(4) **Selection of a conduit/implementer for the funding:** Determination of the program and organization whose mission and funds best qualifies them to execute the project; implementation may be further delegated to host nation (HN) entities.

(5) **Assignment of project administration and oversight**: The management of the project and compliance with regulatory mechanisms.

(6) **Delivery to the end user (recipient) and assessment**: Monitoring and evaluation (M&E), the degree to which project resources are expended and objectives are met.

b. Figure I-1 provides a high-level depiction of the IFO model. Although it depicts the six steps and the key interrelationships as an aid to understanding, the connections are often complex with multiple dependencies. The model depicts progression from project evaluation, through funding, approval, implementation, oversight, and delivery

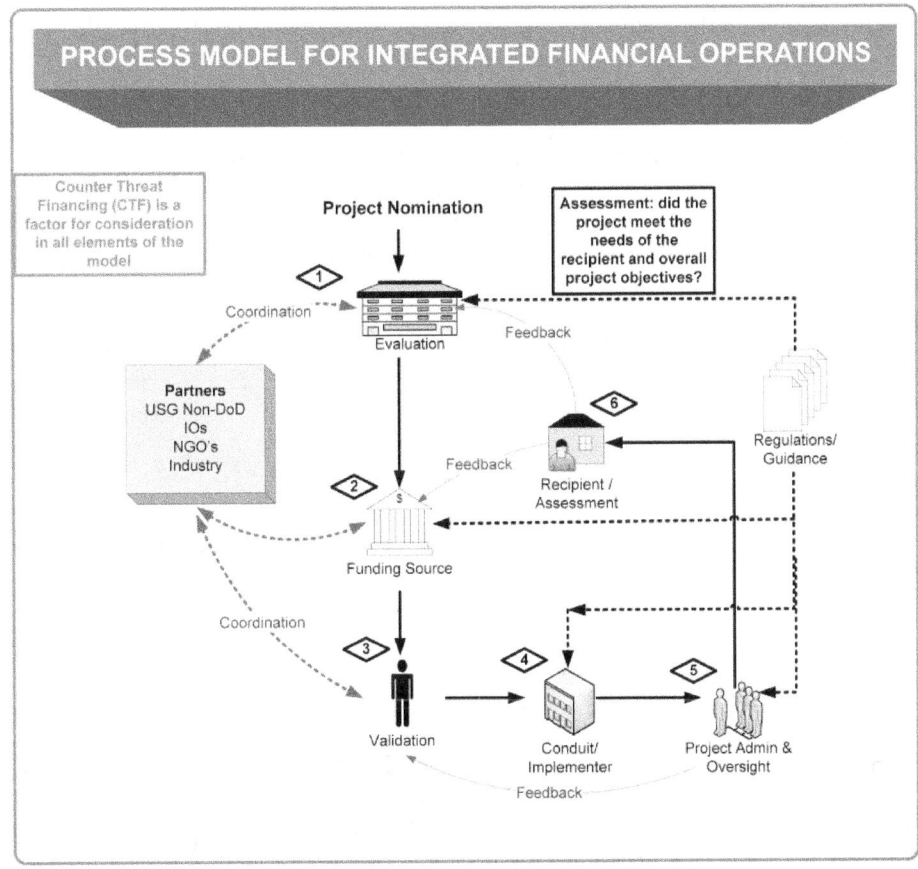

Figure I-1. Process Model for Integrated Financial Operations

as linear; however, in practice the process will be complicated and could involve multiple iterations.

c. The process commences with an evaluation of a project's requirements and its anticipated benefits. Experience in Afghanistan indicates that nominations may come from multiple sources; bottom-up from the provincial reconstruction teams (PRTs) or a local HN official; or, top down, from the highest levels of the USG. This submission of requirements is a multifaceted process that lacks standardization and an efficient means of prioritization. Requests for funding must be evaluated (Step 1). Unfortunately, common criteria and a standardized method to evaluate requirements are not always utilized, even if available. Identification of funding sources (Step 2) requires an understanding of the alternatives both within the military chain (e.g., Commander's Emergency Response Program (CERP)), and those external to DOD, such as USAID's Economic Support Fund (ESF).

d. Validation (Step 3) requires compilation of the assessments completed in the evaluation step into a submission that contains adequate detail for approval. Additionally, the submission must confirm compliance with existing criteria for the funding source. Project approval authority is normally dependent upon the amount of the funding requested and may be conducted at various levels. Once approved, the project must be implemented (Step 4). A variety of options for project execution, i.e., who actually performs the work, is available, each with its own advantages, risks, and drawbacks. In many cases, the preferred option is to use local HN assets whenever possible. In an area with geographically dispersed projects, administration and oversight (Step 5) of the project requires specialized skills that may not be readily available at the construction site. In an uncertain or hostile environment, the difficulties in on-scene oversight are exacerbated. Finally, some means of assessment and feedback (Step 6) into the process must take place, i.e., did the project meet the needs of the recipient and complete the stated objectives.

e. Additionally, the project results must be assessed against the overall joint operation/campaign objectives, i.e., did the project make the desired contribution to the attainment of operational objectives. Effective assessment requires the determination of measures for monitoring and evaluation early in the process.

f. Compliance with regulations and policy mandates is an essential part of each element, and similarly there will be CTF considerations during each process step. For example; evaluation, approval, and especially selection of the implementer must carefully consider the CTF implications, so that the project does not contribute to the adversary's financial networks. CTF can allow the JFC to deny insurgents access to vital funding streams by identifying the sources and conduits of funding and which insurgent elements utilize them. CTF can provide valuable intelligence to operators if intelligence collectors are sufficiently aware of CTF to recognize useful financial intelligence when they see it. This includes financial document exploitation and providing appropriate instructions for authorized collectors of intelligence on how to obtain CTF-related information. Such information could help prevent US funds from inadvertently flowing to the insurgencies and allow operators to target or capture insurgents involved in illicit financial activities.

g. Each process step has a set of tasks. These will vary based on a multiplicity of factors, including the specific effect the project is designed to achieve, the operational environment, scope of the project, and the funding to be utilized. However, those outlined below are appropriate for application to most perceived IFO related projects.

4. Capabilities and Requirements for Conducting Integrated Financial Operations

"We will focus on communities to drive a wedge between the insurgents and the people and give the people the freedom and a reason to support the Afghan government. At the same time, we will continue to invest in critical infrastructure and service delivery systems critical to the development of sustainable national governance and economic growth. Our efforts must be balanced in order to ensure capacity is built to be sustainable and mutually supporting from the local village to the provincial center to Kabul."

USG Integrated Civilian-Military Campaign Plan for Support to Afghanistan, August 2009

a. The above statement clearly and concisely describes the objectives of IFO in an operational area. While certain elements of IFO are unique, many of the capabilities and requirements for its execution are defined elsewhere. For example, the *Handbook for Military Support to Economic Stabilization* states that supporting economic stabilization represents enabling the economic conditions that usher in the nascent stages of growth that allow for the resumption of commercial activities. These conditions include re-opening and operating businesses, the increase of, or the reversal of, downward trends in private sector employment, and reestablishing or maintaining functioning markets.[7] The term, "capability," as defined by JP 1-02, *Department of Defense Dictionary of Military and Associated Terms*, is "the ability to execute a specified course of action. A capability may or may not be accompanied by an intention."[8] A JFC must attain specific capabilities to effectively plan, execute, and assess financial operations. These include the ability to:

(1) Leverage money and contracting assets that contribute to joint operation/campaign objectives;

(2) Engage constructively other individuals/organizations operating in the same locations and/or the same sectors;

(3) Redesign requests to optimize outcomes, impact, and sustainability;

(4) Identify and leverage funding for related activities from other sources;

(5) Engage and obtain local buy-in and community contributions;

(6) Identify valid, reliable, and achievable indicators and benchmarks and have them accessible to all concerned parties responsible for the monitoring and assessment of projects;

(7) Conduct evaluations in the immediate activity end-period and at subsequent points after the activity's end; and

(8) Capture the results in a database for use by others in future activity requests and designs.

b. A requirement, also known as a military requirement or operational requirement as defined by JP 1-02 is, "an established need justifying the timely allocation of resources to achieve a capability to accomplish approved military objectives, missions, or tasks."[9] Leaders must have the requisite knowledge regarding funding programs and contracting to enable them to leverage the use of money in the conduct of operations. Additionally, proactive leadership involvement is critical to reducing the potential for fraud, waste, and abuse of funds.[10] Hence, it is essential that JFCs and their staffs understand the process and fully integrate financial operations into their planning activities. Research during development of this handbook revealed some additional specific requirements for employment of IFO as follows:

(1) Awareness of past, ongoing, and planned projects;

(2) A viable process for getting requirements into the system;

(3) Access to current criteria for submission and evaluation;

(4) Awareness of high-level strategic guidance;

(5) Awareness of all potential funding sources;

(6) Awareness of regulations and directives related to funding sources;

(7) Fully trained and capable personnel;

(8) Common metrics and a process or guidelines that enable effective assessment; and

(9) Access to current criteria for evaluation including the use of CTF resources to ensure that when funds are allocated, they are not falling into the hands of individuals aiding and abetting the enemy.

c. Attainment of the aforementioned capabilities and satisfaction of these requirements would certainly enhance the ability of a JFC to conduct IFO. However, many gaps or shortfalls have been identified.

5. Shortfalls in Effectively Employing Integrated Financial Operations

a. Shortfalls in the ability to achieve the requirements outlined above include:

(1) Insufficient ability to obtain and maintain situational awareness and transparency of all ongoing financial operations;

(2) Inadequate understanding of complex multiple funding sources and complex processes;

(3) Inconsistency in the approval process;

(4) A lack of effective metrics;

(5) Inability to provide oversight and monitoring of ongoing stabilization or development projects; and

(6) Insufficient assessment procedures to determine if completed projects are contributing to the accomplishment of the joint operation/campaign objectives.

b. This handbook addresses the problem of integration, synchronization, prioritization, and targeting of fiscal resources and capabilities with the related efforts of interagency and multinational partners and NGOs against the insurgency, and in support of the population, combined with an ability to exploit and destroy an enemy's financial networks. As a means of mitigating the adverse effects of the identified shortfalls, it introduces changes needed to plan and execute IFO. To this end, this handbook describes a process and organizational solution that could provide the JFC with the ability to use financial operations as an integral part of attaining joint operation/campaign objectives.

c. Subsequent chapters of this handbook will address the key elements of IFO implementation at the operational level.

(1) **Chapter II, "Planning Considerations."** This chapter addresses development of courses of action, and leveraging partners and stakeholders in financial operations. It presents brief examinations of the key partners in IFO and the implications of coordinating with various contributors, including other USG agencies, multinational partners, IGOs, and NGOs operating within the operational area. Additionally, this chapter presents mechanisms currently in use for technical coordination of financial operations, introduces interactions with CTF, and describes an organizational structure appropriate for planning, execution, and assessment of IFO.

(2) **Chapter III, "Assessment and Implications for Employment of Integrated Financial Operations."** Recognizing that assessment is an extremely difficult process, this chapter will identify assessment guidelines and best practices that exist throughout the development community. Different organizations' goals will, at times, conflict; however, the establishment of common operational objectives, through the integration of financial operations under a common joint operation/campaign plan, should reduce this problem. This chapter will then address the body of research available regarding the efficacy of stabilization and development efforts. No effort, however, is made to evaluate, assess or adjudicate how, when, and where development dollars should be spent. The purpose of this section is to provide a framework of analysis that can be applied when considering financial operations.

(3) **Chapter IV, "Training."** This chapter will identify the various training courses and venues currently available for individuals who might find themselves involved in multiple-source financial operations. It will also make recommendations on how to improve current training and education in support of IFO.

CHAPTER II
PLANNING CONSIDERATIONS

"Joint Force Commanders and staffs should consider how to involve relevant government agencies and other nonmilitary organizations in the planning process and how to integrate and synchronize joint force actions with the operations of these agencies. Regardless of the level of involvement by nonmilitary agencies during the planning process, commanders and staffs must consider their impact on joint operations."

JP 5-0, Joint Operation Planning

1. Introduction

a. IFO are inherently complex, but they can increase momentum in an operational area. Financial operations can include direct funding using currency, business processes, networks of stocks and/or specific goods and services of value. Ultimately, IFO seeks to increase the effectiveness of all resources spent in an operational area. Based on findings of the Special Inspectors General for Afghanistan Reconstruction and for Iraq Reconstruction, it is clear that when financial operations are not integrated in an operational area, it can lead to contractor inefficiency, unnecessary and duplicative spending, and even the inadvertent funding of the insurgency. Employment of IFO confronts the JFC with the challenge of gaining situational awareness across a myriad of organizations and their activities not under the JFC's command and then leveraging those efforts to achieve joint operation/campaign objectives.

b. To coordinate and leverage efforts in the operational area effectively, the JFC and their staffs need to fully integrate financial operations into the Joint Operation Planning Process (JOPP). During mission analysis, the goal is to understand the purpose of the operation and issue appropriate guidance to drive the rest of the planning process after the identification of the operational objectives and desired effects. Operational objectives should be tied to one or more higher level objectives, be unambiguous, but should not specify in detail the ways and means for accomplishment of the objective. A desired effect is the physical and/or behavioral state that results from actions taken. It is designed to help the JFC and their staffs determine the conditions that need to exist to achieve objectives. Financial operations are assets that use economic elements of national power to stabilize an area and promote its political and economic development. They are additional tools available to the JFC to create the desired effects and, ultimately, achieve the commander's objectives.

c. To develop a course of action (COA), the JFC needs to know:

(1) What type of action will occur?

(2) What is the purpose of the action and the logistics of the action?

(3) Who will be involved in the action?

(4) When will the action begin?

(5) Where will the action occur?

(6) How will the action occur?

d. These aspects need to be determined before a COA can be converted to a Concept of Operations (CONOPS). However, IFO creates several challenges in this approach, because determining the logistics and timing of actions involves coordination with the various agencies and organizations that are involved in financial operations within the operational area, but not under the JFC's command authority. When implementing financial operations, it is critical that the ongoing efforts of other organizations and agencies are factored into the COA. Conducting financial operations independent of other participants in the operational area leads to stove-piping, redundancy, contractor inefficiency, and ultimately an ineffective means to achieve the larger national and more specific operational objectives.[11]

2. Developing a Course of Action: Leveraging Partners and Stakeholders

a. Strategic and operational objectives of DOD organizations tend not to coincide with the goals and objectives of non-DOD organizations and are not transparent to other organizations conducting operations within an operational area. IFO calls for visibility and coordination of the multiple ongoing stability and development efforts in a given operational area and the organizations undertaking them. Visibility refers to situational awareness of ongoing financial operations efforts in the operational area by all parties.

b. Improved awareness begins with recognizing the financial footprint in the operational area. Mere presence and the meeting of military requirements to carry out operations, such as contracting with local businesses to provide support to forward operating bases (FOBs) (e.g. fuel, trash disposal), changes the local political and economic dynamic. IFO injects additional money into an environment that may or may not have the capacity to absorb it. Dollars spent supporting FOBs, especially large FOBs, can alter local economic and political power structures, sometimes more than targeted projects meant to influence the population. This does not entail subordination of requirements by such considerations; however, the JFC needs to recognize financial operations often begin with the simple arrival of military forces in the operational area. This is particularly true in Iraq and Afghanistan.[12]

c. Additionally, visibility includes identifying the organizations expending funds in a given operational area, their objectives, sources of funding, capabilities, and how they conduct operations. Gathering and understanding this information will move the JFC and staffs towards coordination with other organizations in the operational area. Depending on the location, the JFC may find needed information on other organizations from the US Embassy, the mission director of United States Agency for International Development (USAID) in the region (if appointed), the NGOs who receive USG funding, or interagency partners at the PRT (or similar) level.

d. Coordination of IFO efforts requires extensive effort, which has two parts; synchronization and deconfliction. Synchronization is the arrangement of military actions in time, space, and purpose to produce maximum relative combat power at a decisive place and time. Specific expertise or capabilities could make those implementing partners the best choice to achieve an IFO-related objective or offset a capabilities gap. Deconfliction is avoiding duplication of effort by USG and international contributors, as well as preventing the USG and international stakeholders from working at cross purposes in the operational area. By synchronizing military efforts with other partners, a set of mutual objectives can be recognized, to motivate meaningful coordination. Achieving coordination at any level for financial operations requires an understanding of the types of activities that should be coordinated and the mechanisms and applicable guidance already in existence.[13]

e. Because the solution to a problem when conducting military operations, seldom, if ever, resides within the capability of just one organization, joint operation/campaign plans must be crafted to recognize the core competencies of various agencies and military activities must be coordinated and resources integrated with those of others to achieve the operational objectives. Recent operations in both Iraq and Afghanistan have clearly shown there will not be a single authority over civilian USG agencies with clearly defined roles and responsibilities (i.e., unity of command). At best, "unity of effort" may be achieved. Coordinating and integrating efforts between the joint force and USG agencies, multinational partners, IGOs, and NGOs (which include the for-profit private sector), cannot and should not be equated to the command and control (C2) of a military operation. Non-military stakeholders do not have similarly sized resources nor the same mission and reporting requirements. More critically, their perspectives on a situation and possible solutions are different and the different professional cultures can sometimes clash.

f. These differences present significant coordination challenges. However, the commander should be aware and recognize that these other agencies often possess far greater expertise, and in some cases, more capabilities than the military to execute political, diplomatic, and economic missions. JP 3-08 states, "the degree to which military and civilian components can be integrated and harmonized will bear directly on efficiency and success." Hence, it is imperative for financial operations that partners in the operational area to be included, whenever possible, in the planning process.

g. A mutual understanding of organizational goals, processes, and procedures is critical for successful IFO. Integration among all the organizations involved in financial operations will improve coordination that should result in greater synchronization and prioritization. Clearly, this two-way street will allow civilian partners such as the Department of State (DOS) and USAID to provide input into proposed military projects. Some organizations working in the operational area may have separate reporting chains and cannot or will not directly support the JFC in the planning and execution of the joint operation/campaign plan. However, if the methodology suggested within this guide is implemented, the majority of the stabilization and development efforts in the operational area will be integrated and, consequently, more effective.

h. In most permissive environments, such as Combined Joint Task Force- Horn of Africa (CJTF-HOA), DOD elements are the supporting organization and USG, international, and other organizations will be the supported element. This does not reduce the need to incorporate financial operations into all joint operation/campaign plans to fully leverage all the elements of national power. The objectives of all USG organizations, including the military, should be nested within the strategic goals of the United States.

i. Along with an understanding of other organizational goals and lead roles, there is the recognition of general differences in the cultures of organizations. Generally, in cases where the military has a supporting role to the DOS and USAID, there is a tendency for the military to present already pre-formulated plans. US national policy dictates DOS has the leading role in stability operations. The JFC is, in these operations, confronted with the challenge of assuming the role of a partner. The JFC must also recognize that differences between organizations does not insinuate one is more or less effective than the other, and must put aside such notions, instead adjusting military culture to other organizations, when possible. For instance, while the military favors briefings with slides, DOS prefers to discuss and draw out plans together as opposed to being briefed.[14] Understanding the differences in the cultures of DOS and DOD will enable a better reconciliation of roles and produce greater coordination and collaboration for IFO. Other organization goals, differences, and processes (not limited to DOS and USAID) are discussed below in Paragraph 3, "Organizational Coordination."

j. Currently, Afghanistan is the operational area where the US is decisively engaged in stability operations, and potentially the most complex; therefore, it will be used throughout this handbook as a model. Since Afghanistan has its own unique players, processes, and funding streams, these particulars will be further clarified in Appendices A and B, for those currently deployed to that operational area. It is recognized that there will be differences in other operational areas. However, the principles contained in this guide are globally applicable.

3. Financial Operations Stakeholders

a. Several key USG organizations, e.g., DOS and USAID, plan and execute financial operations.[15] The JFC must have situational awareness of their activities and the ability to coordinate with these organizations. Each can play a key role in the civilian-military structure (explained below in Paragraph 5, "Strategic Coordinating Mechanisms"), because each has their own substantial funding streams that are independent of joint force funding. However, they have different and distinct missions to accomplish in the operational area. These organizations may have expertise and capabilities not inherent in DOD, which could help achieve the operational objectives if leveraged properly. The organizations include:

(1) **US Department of State**. DOS works to advance the freedoms of the international community by "helping to build and sustain a more democratic, secure, and prosperous world composed of well-governed states that respond to the needs of their people, reduce widespread poverty, and act responsibly within the international system."[16] DOS performs diplomatic and political reporting and is responsible for the conduct of bi-lateral relationships with foreign countries and multi-national organizations such as the United Nations (UN). It has direct access to nearly all foreign governments through US Embassies.[17] Representatives from nearly every USG organization are attached to the embassy and comprise the Country Team, under the leadership of the Ambassador, to meet, to share information, formally and informally, and to coordinate their efforts within a host country. The Ambassador, or Chief-of-Mission (COM), is the senior US representative and personal envoy of the president in a host country regardless of which agency may have the lead on specific operations. Many organizations within DOS participate in financial operations, either directly managing funds appropriated by Congress or overseeing the policies related to use of those funds.[18] The department's

Office of the Coordinator for Reconstruction and Stabilization (S/CRS) is responsible for COIN and crisis stabilization matters. The mission of S/CRS is to "lead, coordinate, and institutionalize USG civilian capacity to prevent or prepare for post-conflict situations, and to help stabilize and reconstruct societies in transition from conflict or civil strife, so they can reach a sustainable path toward peace, democracy and a market economy."[19] S/CRS is an interagency team staffed by various USG representatives to lead the civilian component, in concert with military forces, in the coordination of stabilization and reconstruction efforts. It includes members from DOS, USAID, Office of the Secretary of Defense (OSD), Central Intelligence Agency (CIA), Army Corps of Engineers, USJFCOM, Joint Chiefs of Staff, and the Treasury Department.[20] In the Afghan operational area, any high-level contact or policy action necessary, with either the Afghan or the Pakistani governments, are generally executed via DOS and the Ambassador's Country Team.[21]

(2) **US Agency for International Development**. USAID is a semi-independent agency that provides economic, development and humanitarian assistance around the world in support of the foreign policy goals of the United States. USAID receives policy guidance and increasingly programmatic direction from DOS. The USAID Administrator leads the agency in Washington, DC, and serves as a Deputy Secretary equivalent. The Administrator's in-country representative is the Mission Director. Sometimes located at the US Embassy, or in their own building, the Mission Director is the one in charge of all USAID activities in each country. DOS does provide foreign policy guidance. USAID is organized into geographic and functional bureaus as well as independent offices. Geographic bureaus manage overall activities within the countries USAID has programs, whereas functional bureaus manage programs that are worldwide or cross borders. USAID is focused on three primary program areas: economic growth, agriculture, and trade; global health; and democracy, conflict prevention, and humanitarian assistance and is the implementing body of most US Foreign Assistance Funds around the globe.

(a) Many USAID personnel are trained and experienced in the conduct of development operations in post-conflict environments. In addition to US foreign service and civil service officers, USAID employs a large number of foreign nationals at overseas missions to help administer its assistance programs. Most programs are implemented through for-profit contractors and not-for-profit grantees. These NGOs are the means through which USAID implements its operations. When operating in a country, military personnel are likely to meet USAID representatives in the capital cities and in PRTs.

(b) USAID operates on a different planning horizon than DOD; a condition that is frequently misunderstood. As with all development efforts, USAID operates in a supporting role to foreign governments and communities, as dictated by the pace set by the local population, where progress may be measured in terms of decades or generations rather than year-to-year. When operating closely with military forces, there is justifiable concern that USAID's effectiveness, and that of its implementing partners, not be diminished by local perceptions that they are engaged in military or intelligence operations. Depending on the operational area, coordination with USAID, its partners, and other development organizations, in a manner consistent with USAID policies and goals.

(c) USAID will not always provide other organizations (such as the US military) with lists of the local contractors and subcontractors it funds in an operational area for one of two reasons: 1) either USAID does not have the information readily available, or 2) it has a specific reason not to share it. USAID has offices and personnel on the ground in a multitude of countries around the globe, enabling unique connections with local populations over which it is very protective.

(d) USAID receives all of its funding under the Foreign Assistance Act of 1961, which is congressionally approved each year. USAID is one of a very few federal departments and agencies that can receive funds directly from private sources (e.g., corporations and charities) to be used in partnerships.

(3) **Additional US Government Agencies**. Other USG agencies participating in the execution of financial operations include the Department of Agriculture (DOA), Department of Health and Human Services (DHHS), and Department of Education. Agencies supporting CTF efforts include the Department of Justice (DOJ), Department of Treasury (TREAS), Drug Enforcement Administration (DEA), and the CIA.

(4) **United Nations**. The UN's purpose is to maintain international peace and security, develop friendly relations among nations, be the harmonizer of the actions of nations, and achieve international cooperation in "solving international problems of an economic, social, cultural, or humanitarian character, and in promoting and encouraging respect for human rights and for fundamental freedoms for all without distinction as to race, sex, language, or religion."[22] However, in situations where there is conflict or in humanitarian crises, the UN delegates the Office of Coordination and Humanitarian Assistance (OCHA) to lead all of the various UN bodies in the country. OCHA's mission is to mobilize and coordinate effective and principled humanitarian action in partnership with national and international actors in order to alleviate human suffering in disasters and emergencies; advocate for the rights of people in need; promote preparedness and prevention; and facilitate sustainable solutions. In the case of Afghanistan, the UN's Assistance Mission in Afghanistan (UNAMA), with the current mission statement, supports the rebuilding of the country and the strengthening of the foundations of peace and a constitutional democracy. The 2010 resolution recognizes the key role played by the UN in coordinating international efforts in Afghanistan and in supporting the Government of Afghanistan in critical areas, including security, governance, and regional cooperation; as well as supporting the full implementation of mutual commitments made on these issues at the London Conference in January 2010.[23]

(a) UN personnel are highly visible and frequently will not be allowed to operate in an environment if security conditions deteriorate. In Iraq and Afghanistan, insurgents have targeted UN officials resulting in the UN pulling its remaining staff out of the area. The UN also supports country specific aid and development missions; for example, the UN operates UNAMA in Afghanistan and although they are undermanned, they often enjoy good relationships and exchange information with NGOs operating in the operational area. However, UN personnel are cognizant of and sensitive to their neutral status and are sensitive about sharing information with military personnel without the perception of some overriding benefit to their mission.

(b) The Department of Public Information (DPI), established by the UN's Economic and Social Council, acts as a liaison between NGOs, the UN, and other civil society organizations, creating partnerships and providing information services such as briefings, workshops and annual conferences.[24]

(5) **Provincial Reconstruction Team**. PRTs are operated by the International Security Assistance Force (ISAF), under the leadership of the North Atlantic Treaty Organization (NATO). PRTs were first used by the US in 2003 for Operation ENDURING FREEDOM in Afghanistan and since then also used in Iraq. As integrated civilian-military organizations, PRTs are supported by individual donor nations and currently twenty-six PRTs operate in provinces across Afghanistan. They manage teams of international civil–military affairs specialists and often have excellent knowledge of and relationships with local Afghans and local Afghan government officials in their areas of operation. Those PRTs' mission is to support the growth and increased capacity of the HN through securing areas so that reconstruction efforts can proceed, as well as providing support for humanitarian assistance. Teams can be from a single nation or multinational and consist of about eighty people, sixty who are experts in foreign affairs, agriculture, and engineering; while the remaining twenty are civilian specialists who work with Afghan partners.[25]

(a) Projects conducted by US led PRTs use the CERP monies or such other funds as Congress may authorize. CERP requests for large projects must receive the approval of the higher headquarters. Non-US led PRTs do have access to CERP; a majority of the funding comes from their respective nations. For nations that do not provide funds to their PRTs, the funds are received from the UN or the HN. Funds also come from the USAID representative (local governance and community development program (LGCD)) embedded with the PRT. The USAID representative does not have the authority to dispense funds for high cost projects; that must come from certified contracting officers. The local governance and community development fund is the only USAID monies available to the PRTs.[26] At the operational level, the PRTs are vital hubs where civil-military efforts are concentrated before they reach out like spokes to the surrounding local population.

(b) PRTs have a high turnover rate of personnel, but in the case of Afghanistan and Iraq, they are familiar to the local population and often have established relationships with local leaders and communities. PRTs are in a position to access economic data on local districts and provinces that may not be available anywhere else. However, PRTs went from being a means to get into unsecure areas and pave the way for the HN or development agencies, to actually taking on reconstruction projects.[27] The future of PRTs is uncertain. Some PRTs in Afghanistan have undertaken work that could potentially be done by the local entities. Consequently, this has undermined the legitimacy of the Afghan government. PRT commanders cannot meet every local demand. Therefore, they must prioritize their resources. As a result, there are often areas surrounding PRTs where development is non-existent, whereas neighboring districts are awash in foreign assistance. This disparity has, in the case of Afghanistan, created political and social tensions among the populace.

(c) An example of PRT and military coordination is within the US Forces-Iraq operational area, where each PRT has a work plan synchronized with the military's operations plan.[28] The PRTs in Iraq are all coordinated through the US Embassy's Office of Provincial Affairs (OPA). US Forces lend military officers to OPA to assist in the planning and coordinating of activities. The officers are integrated with the OPA staff and actually report to the Director of the OPA.[29]

(6) **Nongovernmental Organizations**. Other stakeholders, such as NGOs and the private sector, directly affect the conduct of operations, including financial operations. Therefore, the JFC requires situational awareness of their activities so that they can be accounted for in joint operation/campaign planning. These groups create unique challenges for the JFC when attempting to gain this situational awareness of their goals and ongoing activities. The United States Institute for Peace, an independent, nonpartisan, national institution, has done extensive work in establishing guidelines for interactions between NGOs and the military. Due to their missions, humanitarian NGOs value neutrality and independence as a key operating principle. Humanitarian organizations are those who provide assistance to those in need regardless of which ideology, religion, or faction is involved. They remain focused on providing needed care and, as a result, normally are not targeted by combatants. If humanitarian organizations are perceived to be working for one side or another in a conflict, they may be targeted or forced to leave the operational area. Therefore, many are keen on preserving what they refer to as "humanitarian space." This means that some humanitarian groups may avoid contact with DOD personnel or refuse to share information, not because they do not want to help the DOD, but because doing so could imperil their mission and personnel's safety. Independence, in this context, is defined as not acting as an instrument of government foreign policy. Guided by their own policies and implementation strategies, they do not seek to implement the policy of any government, except insofar as it coincides with their own independent policies. To maintain independence, they will never knowingly—or through negligence—allow themselves, or their employees, to be used to gather information of a political, military, or economically sensitive nature for governments or other bodies that may serve purposes other than those that are strictly humanitarian, nor will they act as instruments of foreign policy of donor governments.[30] The guidelines referenced above recommend using the following conduits to liaison with NGOs in the operational area:

(a) USAID

(b) S/CRS

(c) The UN OCHA representative could be a strong candidate to serve as liaison because its representative normally would be responsible for working with all NGOs and maintaining contact with the host government or a successor regime. Again, as stated earlier, the JFC and staff must be cognizant and sensitive to the UN's charter and neutrality.

(7) In conclusion, achieving coordination of financial operations requires first an understanding of the coordinating mechanisms and applicable guidance already in existence. A coordinating mechanism can be a strategy or blueprint for action, such as the Afghan National Development Strategy (ANDS), or it can be a working group such as the Provincial Reconstruction and Development Committee. Coordinating mechanisms, technical and strategic, are already operating in Afghanistan and/or other operational areas, as will be discussed in the next sections.

4. Technical Coordinating Mechanisms

a. In order to gain the ability to integrate, synchronize, prioritize, and target fiscal resources and capabilities to achieve operational objectives, the JFC must have adequate situational awareness within the assigned operational area. This includes possessing the knowledge and ability to know at any given time, the different efforts (developmental and stabilizing) that are being proposed or initiated, the status of efforts, personnel/organizations involved with those efforts, important contact points, end results of efforts, and any important warnings regarding suspected corrupt entities or personnel. As pointed out in the 2009 Special Inspector General for Afghanistan Reconstruction (SIGAR) report, there have been consistent oversight concerns related to lack of accountability, inadequate integration of projects, and corruption.[31]

b. Coordinated efforts through technical means are a mechanism to achieve de-confliction and synchronization. For USG agencies, the National Defense Authorization Act (NDAA) for Fiscal Year 2008 (FY08) emphasized the importance of coordination through the memorandum of understanding (MOU) requirement. The MOU mandates the Secretaries of Defense and State, and the Administrator of the USAID to identify common databases to be used for the storage of Iraq and Afghanistan contract-related information. For the purposes of this common database, the elements to be included, must be agreed upon and included in a list of minimums dictated by the NDAA.[32] The list includes:

(1) For each contract that involves work performed in Iraq or Afghanistan for more than 14 days; a brief description of the contract, its total value, and whether it was awarded competitively; and

(2) For contractor personnel working under contracts in Iraq or Afghanistan; total number employed, performing security functions, and killed or wounded.

c. Based on the requirements levied by the NDAA, DOD, DOS, and USAID agreed to use the Synchronized Predeployment and Operational Tracker (SPOT). SPOT is a web-based system that is maintained by DOD. SPOT details Iraq or Afghanistan contracts of more than fourteen days of performance or valued at more than $100,000 with additional information on the contract personnel. Later NDAAs (FY09 and FY10) mandated further information to be included in the database concerning criminal offenses committed by or against contractor personnel[33] and the inclusion of grants and cooperative agreements as part of the definition of contracts. Also, the minimum of fourteen days of performance was extended to thirty days.[34] In the MOU of July 2008, it was agreed that it was the responsibility of each agency to accurately input data. Further, the agencies agreed that contract-related information would be imported to SPOT from the Federal Procurement Data System – Next Generation (FPDS-NG). The direct import from FPDS-NG to SPOT is to be implemented in October 2010. For this to be fully effective, changes in how data, e.g., contract numbers, is entered into SPOT, will need to be standardized so that all data can be linked and provide the user a reliable picture. This capability, when fully implemented, will allow all users to have visibility on the majority of USG money being expended, what projects are currently being executed, and projects planned for the operational area. This should greatly reduce the duplication of effort and contractor inefficiency and is a solution that would provide utility irrespective of responsibility area as SPOT is planned for DOD-wide implementation.

d. There are significant reservations regarding the manner in which data must be entered into SPOT. USAID is reluctant to enter data into a system that includes the identification of local nationals employed in areas such as Afghanistan. Any compromise of the data could endanger those working for the USG.

e. Currently, the Combined Information Data Network Exchange (CIDNE) database is the database of record for significant activities of USFOR-A, to include the execution of projects using CERP. CIDNE endeavors to provide visibility and access data uploaded from Brigade Combat Teams and PRTs in a web-based tool. It is a reporting tool that enables disparate communities to share information through a standardized reporting framework that not only provides information on ongoing projects, it also asks key questions to determine if a proposed project fits within the scope of CERP.[35] It enhances civil affairs missions by sharing knowledge through its engagement tool for tracking people, facilities, and organizations.[36]

f. These technical solutions are available today and have been mandated for use to provide mechanisms for visibility and coordination of stabilization and development projects. While in place, it is apparent they are not being used as intended. The US Government Accountability Office (GAO) Report 10-509T determined that although the use of SPOT was agreed upon by the DOD, DOS, and USAID to fulfill the requirements mandated in the NDAA, it is still not being used by the participating organizations.[37] Interviews with USFOR-A forces revealed that CIDNE is still not considered a fully effective capability. It resides on the Secret Internet Protocol Router Network (SIPRNET) providing limited access to those not in DOD and does not have a great deal of flexibility regarding accessing and extracting data. Enhanced use of SPOT requires a review of the data required to meet the requirements of visibility and coordination while not endangering individuals. Changes should be made to SPOT to accommodate the concerns over the safety of local contractors employed by the USG. While these shortfalls are both organizational and technical for these capabilities, if the shortfalls are addressed, the two capabilities can provide much needed visibility of ongoing efforts and a mechanism for coordination among US stakeholders.

5. Strategic Coordinating Mechanisms

a. **Integrated Civilian–Military Decision-Making Structure**. Mission analysis in joint operational planning requires an analysis of the commander's mission and intent. IFO requires an understanding of the linkage between objectives, effects, and tasks; without which the meeting of operational objectives is not possible. In Afghanistan, both the civilian and military leadership recognize that close collaboration among all parties is required to execute IFO effectively. The Civilian-Military Campaign Plan, co-signed by the US Ambassador to Afghanistan and the Commander of ISAF, establishes policies that provide guidance on collaborative ventures to use civilian and military resources efficiently to achieve objectives.[38] This integrated plan addresses the major stakeholders within the Afghanistan operational area. The goal is the creation of integrated civilian-military teams at the district, provincial and regional levels to reduce stovepipe execution of programs and budgets.[39] The document directs the implementation of a civilian-military decision-making structure that extends from Kabul to the district level in Afghanistan. This guide is applicable to IFO globally. Since Afghanistan provides the most complex and challenging case study, the structures described in this section provide examples for possible application in other operational areas. Described in the Civilian-Military Campaign Plan, it consists of five entities that represent different levels of coordination and decision-making for USG and ISAF in partnership with international community elements operating in Afghanistan. The top-down approach is designed to set and prioritize objectives to promote unity of effort and focus stabilization and development efforts down to the local level. A key effort throughout is assessment to determine if the right tasks are being done to achieve strategic goals and objectives.

(1) **Principals' Group (PG).** The COM and Commander of the International Security Assistance Force (COMISAF)/Regional Commander (CDR) USFOR-A are responsible for final coordination and decision making. They provide civilian-military direction, set priorities, consult on priorities with the Government of the Islamic Republic of Afghanistan (GIRoA), work with other nation partners to address common challenges, and allocate resources to USG elements.

(2) **Executive Working Group (EWG).** This deputies-level senior decision-making body makes policy and decisions regarding the Civilian-Military Campaign Plan based on input from the national-level working groups, regional civilian-military cells and the plans and assessment staff. EWG may also inform issues to be brought to the joint coordination monitoring board. The political military section of the US Embassy provides planning and assessment support for the EWG and national-level working groups and works with planners from key USG departments, agencies and ISAF. Working-level groups are responsible for further development, monitoring and assessment of their respective transformative effect strategy in the Civilian-Military Campaign Plan.

(3) **Regional Integrated Team (IT-R).** This assembly of regional level leadership includes the regional command (RC) commander, the USG RC senior civilian representative (SCR), and various representatives from other USG agencies. The regional-level is responsible for providing support and guidance to its subordinate levels, developing and maintaining the integrated civilian-military plan in the region, assessing progress in their region, allocating resources jointly, and raising key issues for engaging with key international partners.

(4) **Sub-regional Integrated Team (IT-S).** This assembly of sub-regional level leadership includes the commanders of the brigade combat teams (BCT), the USG SCR, and the various representatives from other USG agencies. The sub-regional level is responsible for formulating an integrated civilian-military plan for their area, providing support and guidance to its subordinate levels, assessing progress in their area, allocating resources jointly, raising key issues to the regional-level and engaging with key international partners.

(5) **Provincial Integrated Team (IT-P).** This assembly of international provincial-level leadership includes the commanders of the PRTs, the agri-business development team (ADT), the battalion equivalent, the Afghanistan National Security Forces (ANSF) mentor and partner teams, and the provincial USG civilian lead. The IT-P is primarily implementation focused; however, it also is responsible for jointly providing support and guidance to the district level, for formulating a civilian-military plan for support to Afghanistan at the provincial level, assessing progress and stability in the province, allocating resources jointly, raising key issues to the sub-regional or regional-level as required, and engaging key international and GIRoA partners.

"The intent is that all civ-mil elements that conduct operations or activities in the same district or province coordinate and develop plans, assessments and coordination mechanisms that synchronize the full spectrum of USG organizations, military forces, and international partner efforts as well as NGOs, UN, and the whole range of Afghan partners operating in the area."

USG Integrated Civil-Military Campaign for Support to Afghanistan,
August 2009

b. **Government of the Islamic Republic of Afghanistan (GIRoA)**. HN governmental support is critical. The goal of all US actions in Afghanistan is to assist the Afghan government in increasing its capacity to provide infrastructure and service delivery systems critical to developing sustainable governance and economic growth. Increasing such capacities will lead to popular support for GIRoA and reduced support for the insurgency. To that end, it is critical to work within the framework that has been established by the Afghan government. Some of the elements include:

(1) **The Afghanistan National Development Strategy (ANDS)**. The ANDS is used as the guiding principal for many organizations and stakeholders throughout Afghanistan. The ANDS is an important example because it is the plan endorsed and supported by the GIRoA. Central to COIN efforts in Afghanistan is the establishment of a competent and legitimate Afghan government. GIRoA, Ministry of Rural Rehabilitation and Development (MMRD), ISAF, UNAMA, and the PRTs are some of the organizations that reference the ANDS as one of the guiding principles for their objectives. Familiarity with this document would provide the JFC a greater awareness of the stakeholders in the Afghanistan operational area. The ANDS has been widely advertised to the Afghan public. DOD or US government efforts in the operational area which inadvertently work against ANDS goals or appear not to be in support of it may undermine the legitimacy of GIRoA and are contrary to successful COIN. But the ANDS does come with some caveats; it is an enormous document and so vaguely written that just about any project could be interpreted as supporting the ANDS. The current version of the ANDS, valid through 2013, lays out a vision for Afghanistan well through 2020. The pillars and goals of the ANDS are:

(a) **Security**: Achieve nationwide stabilization, strengthen law enforcement, and improve personal security for every Afghan.

(b) **Governance, Rule of Law, and Human Rights**: Strengthen democratic processes and institutions, human rights, the rule of law, delivery of public services and government accountability.

(c) **Economic and Social Development**: Reduce poverty, ensure sustainable development through a private-sector-led market economy, improve human development indicators, and make significant progress towards the millennium development goals (MDGs).

A further vital and cross-cutting area of work is eliminating the narcotics industry, which remains a formidable threat to the people and state of Afghanistan, the region, and beyond.[40]

(2) Though the ANDS is an important document for all organizations involved in the rebuilding of Afghanistan, it does not provide useful information on prioritizing projects. Recently, during the London Conference of 2010, the international community met with GIRoA to renew their commitment to establishing a secure Afghan government. In an effort to ensure better coordinated development, GIRoA is developing a work plan to better refine the ANDS development priorities of agriculture and rural development, human resource development, and infrastructure and economic development. By adopting a clusters approach, whereby key ministries are aligned into development and governance clusters, the ministerial leadership is tasked with prioritizing the implementation of ANDS. These clusters will improve coordination, effectiveness of resource application, and planning. GIRoA requests that donor nations support the clusters through collaboration at technical and financial levels. One of the main goals of GIRoA and the donor nations is to increase the Afghan government's capabilities so that it is able to meet the needs of its people. To do so, GIRoA must develop its own institutions and resources. Currently, the Afghan government's operating expenditures are 35% foreign assistance. The Afghan government wishes to legitimize itself in the eyes of the Afghan people by taking the lead on aid. GIRoA prefers donors provide funds directly to the Afghan government, so that Afghan capacity will increase and sustainability can be ensured, while also increasing accountability by implementing effective monitoring and evaluation systems.[41] In terms of Afghanistan, the JFC and staff would do well to be mindful of the cluster strategy, and attempt to implement projects that coincide with the cluster priorities. The main point to take away from this particular example, is the importance of involving the HN and factoring it into the list of organizations that are involved in the operational area.

(3) **National Solidarity Program (NSP).** NSP was created in 2003 by the Ministry of Rural Rehabilitation and Development to develop the ability of Afghan communities to identify, plan, manage, and monitor their own development projects. Through the promotion of good local governance, the NSP works with 22,000 rural communities in Afghanistan to determine decisions affecting their own lives and livelihoods. A key initiative, it supports decision making and resource allocation at the community level, which is where power in Afghanistan has traditionally resided. Community leaders are a diverse group, and in the southern and eastern regions, it is not uncommon for leaders to put the good of their own tribe or family ahead of the overall community; the Taliban has exploited this shortcoming, claiming in its information campaign that the Taliban represents a force for law and order against the corrupt community leaders supported by NSP. When one tribe, or family, rules the community and allocates resources to its own, rival tribes often feel short changed and the Taliban will intercede and offer support to the rivals, who often accept. This is one such way corruption fuels the insurgency and works against civilian-military efforts.

(a) In support of the NSP, thousands of community development councils (CDCs) were established throughout most provinces and districts of the GIRoA. The main objective of the CDCs is to provide much needed services to local communities until such time as local governments are capable of providing comprehensive support to the local population.

In some cases, funds are provided directly to the CDCs, which create the perception in Afghans minds that CDCs and local governments are legitimate, while the national government in Kabul is corrupt or illegitimate.

(b) On the positive side, allowing community leaders to distribute resources is more effective in terms of identifying and solving local problems. In Afghanistan, local governments are more trusted by Afghans and are therefore a place to build good governance from the ground up.[42] This is where ground up approaches such as CERP and PRTs should coordinate with GIRoA on funding projects and development efforts. With this coordination, should come outward displays of the alliances between CDCs and GIRoA to bolster GIRoA legitimacy.

(4) **Provincial Reconstruction and Development Committee (PRDC)**. The PRDC is a component of the provincial governance structure in both Iraq and Afghanistan. The PRDC consists of 35-40 members who meet in the provincial capital once a week to discuss issues and policy. Once a month, the committee reports to the provincial council regarding the reconstruction projects that have been nominated and approved.

6. Coordinating Counter Threat Finance

a. In accordance with section 113 of Title 10, United States Code, DOD Directive 5205.14, *DoD Counter Threat Finance (CTF) Policy*, dated 19 Aug 10, establishes DOD policy and assigns DOD responsibilities for the conduct of CTF. CTF is the means to detect, counter, contain, disrupt, deter, or dismantle the transnational financing of state and non-state adversaries threatening U.S. national security. Monitoring, assessing, analyzing, and exploiting financial information are key support functions for CTF activities. CTF is not operational area specific; because it looks at the flow of money across several operational areas, it is a global effort not just a regional one. CTF activities include, but are not limited to, countering narcotics trafficking, proliferation activities, WMD networks, trafficking in persons, weapons trafficking, precursor chemical smuggling, terrorist revenue and logistics, anti-corruption, and other such activities that generate revenue through illicit networks. It is critical for those conducting CTF to maintain a strong link with financial execution elements. For example, in Afghanistan, insurgent and criminal elements have been receiving funds from coalition or even USG sources because those executing funds in the operational area did not know which contractors or companies had criminal or insurgent ties. CTF operators have that information and need to get it to those executing IFO before contracts are approved and funded.

b. CTF can allow the JFC to deny insurgents access to vital funding streams by identifying the sources and conduits of funding along with which insurgent elements utilize them. If integrated into the overall visibility of IFO, it provides the JFC more data directed to enemy activities and action can be taken to deny the enemy not only access to funding, but deny the enemy the ability to conduct operations in the operational area. CTF can provide valuable intelligence to operators if intelligence collectors are aware of CTF sufficiently enough to recognize the usefulness of financial intelligence. This includes financial document exploitation and providing appropriate instructions for authorized collectors of intelligence on how to obtain CTF-related information. Such information could help prevent US funds from inadvertently flowing to the insurgencies and allow operators to target or capture insurgents involved in illicit financial activities.

c. CTF can contribute to COIN by eliminating insurgent funding and identifying host government corruption. A legitimate host government is vital to successful COIN. While protection of sources and methods is always an important consideration, a host government often cannot effectively deal with corruption because it lacks hard data on which to build cases against corrupt officials. The dilemma for the JFC in sharing corruption-fighting information with a host government is that it can allow corrupt officials to discover potential action being taken against them. Not sharing information on corrupt officials likely will allow them to continue their illicit activities. Further, targeting or arrests by non-HN authorities can further erode the host government's legitimacy in the eyes of the population.

d. Effective IFO requires sharing of data between those entities specializing in CTF and financial executors. Examples of data sharing that CTF entities could provide are information on possible front companies and individuals and financial organizations with both legitimate and illegitimate business interests to ensure coalition funds are not unwittingly being used to finance the insurgency. Those who are executing funds, such as contracting commands and USAID, collect information, including vendor databases, audit information on specific companies and vendor employee lists which would likely be of value to the CTF stakeholders in their efforts to disrupt the enemy's financial networks. This type of information could also enhance CTF anti-corruption efforts, a growing concern in Afghanistan.

e. CTF is a consideration in all steps of the IFO process described in Chapter I. CTF should be a primary concern in evaluation of projects, selection of conduits or implementers, and assessment. The information derived in this process from a variety of sources can contribute to the knowledge base required for effective CTF.

7. Operational Coordinating Mechanism

a. **Key Implications**. The perceived advantages of participation in an IFO coordinating mechanism by member organizations are an important factor in maximizing cooperation and mutual benefit. Partners will participate only if there is benefit to their own objectives. Development of a "win-win" situation will produce advantages in increased information sharing and cooperation. The JFC, when organizing to conduct IFO, must consider several key implications.

(1) **There is no "one-size-fits-all" membership in the IFO organization**. The structure must account for different levels of involvement when designing the guidelines for the organization responsible for financial operations. The time horizon of projects and individual organizational objectives may require participants to move in and out of the CMOC depending on the level of activity/interest.

(2) **Terms of reference need to be in place early in the process**. Roles, responsibilities and expectations need to be defined upfront to avoid participants coming to the table with unrealistic expectations. The terms of reference must create a mutually beneficial situation for all participants or membership will quickly diminish if they do not see the value of their organization's participation.

(3) **Different structures and leadership relationships should be considered depending on the operational environment**. The JFC should consider different

management/leadership structures (e.g. civilian, military or co-lead) in order to improve the effectiveness of this body responsible for financial operations in the JTF. Personality of the lead is extremely important and he/she must contend with organizational and cultural differences.

b. **Adapting the Civil-Military Operations Center (CMOC)**. JP 5-0, *Joint Operation Planning*, asserts that joint planning integrates military actions with those of other instruments of national power and our multinational partners in time, space, and purpose to achieve a specified end state. Since IFO will integrate the efforts of disparate organizations, a means of applying the elements of the IFO process in this complex environment is required. Therefore, structures and processes that reflect this condition emerge as most appropriate to the planning, execution and assessment of IFO. JP 3-57, *Civil Military Operations*, and JP 3-08 are germane, since the best practices developed for interagency coordination are particularly applicable to IFO. A structure described in JP 3-08, the civil-military operations center (CMOC), provides a means of overcoming the significant challenges of operating with multiple organizational cultures, histories, and objectives; and incorporating IFO into the joint planning process. Although doctrinally the CMOC is not restricted to any specific operational level, most of its previous employments have been primarily at the tactical level. Therefore, its perception as a tactical level construct must be considered. Recognizing its existing connotations, this handbook advocates an IFO coordinating capability based on the CMOC construct. JFCs will use CMOC, or other titles, for their organization. The JFC could elect to utilize a joint interagency coordination group or other boards, bureaus, centers, cells and working groups for the conduct of IFO. The more important factors are the roles, responsibilities, and functions of the organization for planning, execution, and assessment of IFO, not its name. The discussions that follow will use "CMOC" as a title, with the understanding that the name of the construct is not fixed or mandated.

(1) The CMOC is a mechanism that can serve as the primary coordination interface for operational and tactical level coordination between the JFC and other stakeholders. A CMOC may include representatives of US military forces, other USG agencies, multinational partners, IGOs, NGOs, and the private sector. The CMOC is the methodology US forces generally utilize to organize for CMO. A CMOC is a coordinating body and generally neither sets policy nor conducts operations. The organization of the CMOC is theater- and mission-dependent—flexible in size and composition. A JFC at any echelon may establish a CMOC to facilitate coordination with other agencies, departments, organizations, and the HN.

(2) Conceptually, the CMOC is the meeting place of stakeholders. In reality, the CMOC may be physical or virtual and conducted collaboratively through online networks. More than one CMOC may be established in an operational area, and each is task organized based on the mission. The CMOC forum appeals to NGOs and IGOs because it provides these organizations a single-point of coordination with the military for their needs, ensuring that the unified efforts of a joint force and the other organizations are focused when and where they are most needed. A JFC cannot direct interagency cooperation among engaged agencies. However, working together at the CMOC on issues like security, logistic support, information sharing, communications, and other items can build a cooperative spirit among all participants.

(3) As JP 3-08 contends, the creation of a framework for structured civil-military interaction, such as a CMOC, allows the military and NGOs to meet and work together in advancing common goals. Taskings to support IGOs and NGOs are normally for a short-term purpose due to extraordinary events. In most situations, logistics, communications, and security are the capabilities most needed. It is, however, crucial to remember that in such missions the role of the armed forces should be to enable, not perform, IGO and NGO tasks. Military commanders and other decision makers should also understand that mutually beneficial arrangements between the armed forces and other organizations may be critical to the success of the campaign or operation plan.

(4) The CMOC is designed principally for CMO missions. However, its principles may be adapted for use in the IFO context. Figure II-1 depicts a notional CMOC composition.

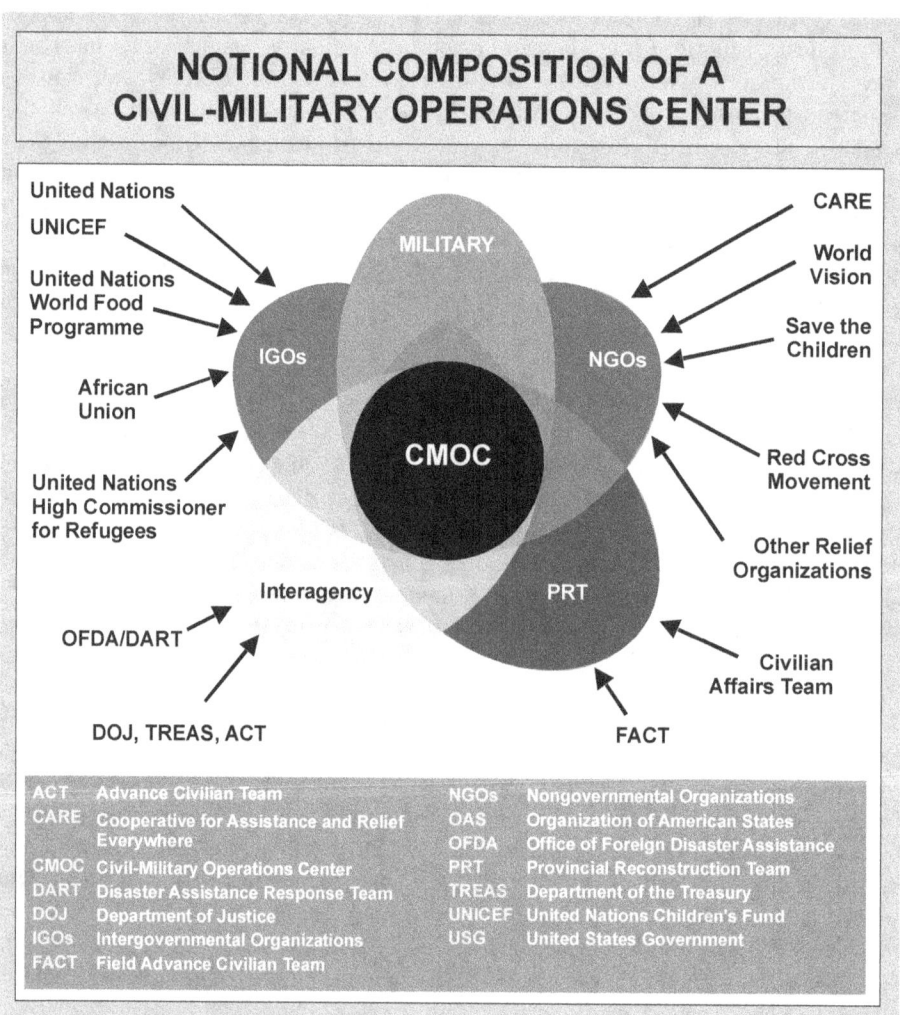

Figure II-1. Notional Composition of a Civil-Military Operations Center

(5) The CMOC is an appropriate structure for IFO due to the similarity CMO functions. Among the activities performed by a CMOC are:

(a) Providing nonmilitary agencies with a focal point for activities and matters that are civilian related;

(b) Receiving, validating, coordinating, and monitoring requests for routine and emergency military support;

(c) Coordinating requests to nonmilitary agencies for their support;

(d) Convening ad hoc mission planning groups to address complex military missions that support nonmilitary requirements;

(e) Coordinating efforts with US or multinational commands, UN, HN, and other nonmilitary agencies;

(f) Facilitating and coordinating activities of the joint force, other on-scene agencies, and higher echelons in the military chain of command;

(g) Coordinating the response to requests for military support with Service components;

(h) Coordinating with USAID; and

(i) Convening follow-on assessment groups.

(6) The vision is for the CMOC to become a USG interagency body, with connections to multinational partners, IGOs, and NGOs; which supports the planning, execution, and assessment of IFO in a joint headquarters. Issues include, but are not limited to, the specific roles, responsibilities, composition, authorities, and knowledge management (KM) requirements that would be required to create this capability within a joint force HQ. Although each JFC will adapt the structure to a specific operational environment and mission, this guide presupposes that some organizations and some skill-sets would be common to most applications. These organizations include the:

(a) Services;

(b) components;

(c) USAID;

(d) DOJ;

(e) Treasury Department;

(f) representatives from partner nations;

(g) IGOs, e.g., UN, NATO, African Union;

(h) NGOs; and,

(i) HN.

(7) Subject matter expertise in related areas is also part of the CMOC composition. These areas include:

(a) contracting,

(b) development

(c) stability operations,

(d) CTF,

(e) legal,

(f) COIN operations,

(g) USG interagency cooperation, and

(h) NGO interface.

(8) Representation may be dedicated or part-time. Only a liaison officer, with no decision-making authority, will represent some organizations. Others may possess full authority to make commitments for their organizations. Geographic co-location of all CMOC members is not a priority requirement. Experience indicates that many civilian organizations and most NGOs will not enter a military headquarters. They will be very cautious about potential perceptions regarding their association with the military. Inherently, the concept will develop a reliable and accessible means of communication between its members.

(9) Conducting the interagency coordination required for IFO requires a departure from traditional military thinking. The legacy requirement for C2 is not appropriate for operational structures and environments where the military commander does not possess clear authority over all activities in the assigned operational area. As a result, coordination and collaboration are more applicable to gaining unity of effort. As with all interagency activities, effective IFO will require inclusion, vice exclusion, of external stakeholders that mandates an understanding of the different roles, authorities, missions, culture and processes of external stakeholders. Due to the inclusive nature of IFO, a rigid hierarchical structure is not appropriate. One of the benefits of the CMOC-like structure is that it is exceptionally flexible and designed to conform to the needs of the JTF. Hence, the specific composition of the CMOC will be based on the requirements of the individual JFC. Importantly, the level of the authority of the JFC is limited. Figure II-2 depicts the various levels of influence a military commander has in a structure that includes non-DOD elements.

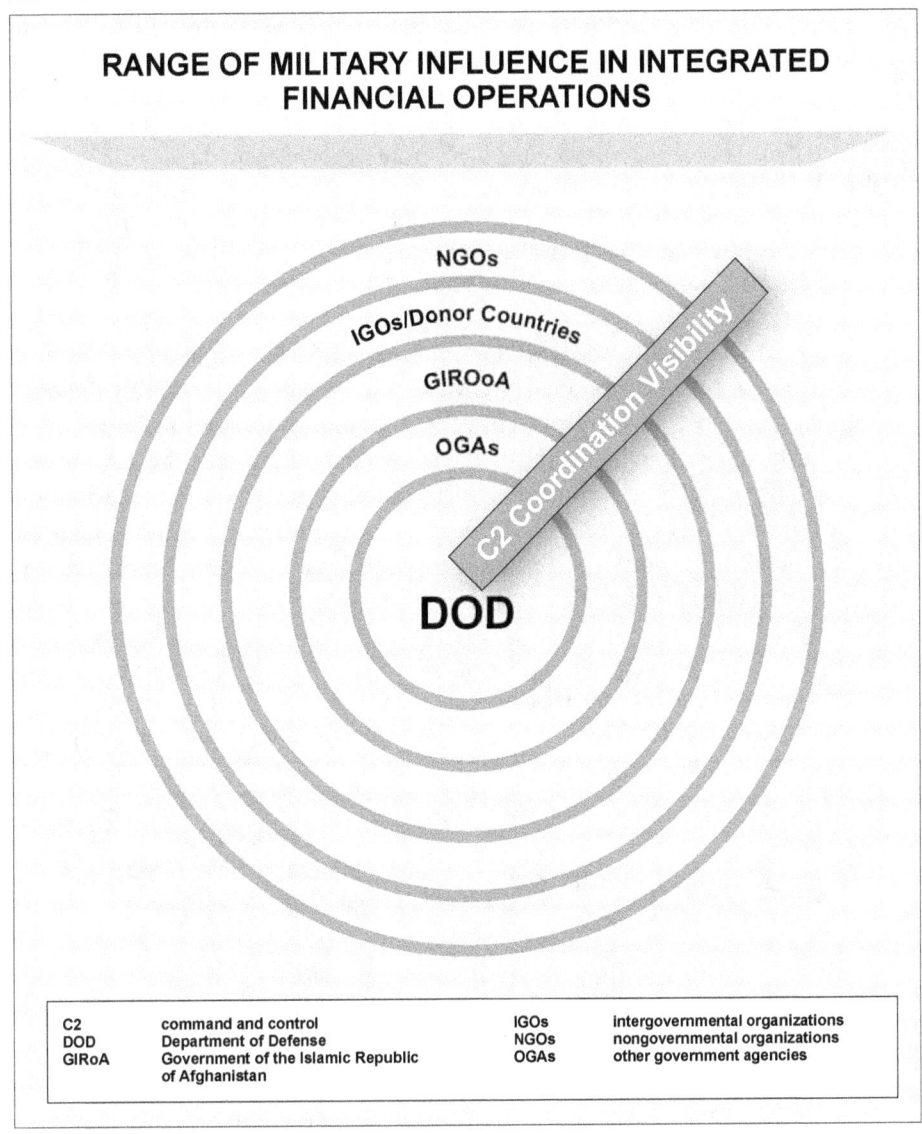

RANGE OF MILITARY INFLUENCE IN INTEGRATED FINANCIAL OPERATIONS

NGOs

IGOs/Donor Countries

GIROoA

OGAs

C2 Coordination Visibility

DOD

C2	command and control	IGOs	intergovernmental organizations
DOD	Department of Defense	NGOs	nongovernmental organizations
GIRoA	Government of the Islamic Republic of Afghanistan	OGAs	other government agencies

Figure II-2. Range of Military Influence in Integrated Financial Operations

(10) While the JFC can exercise command authority over assigned and attached forces, outside DOD, participating organizations will not reflect "unity of command" with one single authority and clearly defined roles and responsibilities. At various times, the JFC draws on the capabilities of other USG agencies, provides capabilities to other organizations, or merely de-conflicts joint force activities with those of others. The JFC may have some form of supported or supporting relationships with IGOs; however, in some operations, USG agencies' relationships with IGOs are voluntary and based upon shared goals and good will. The relationship between the JFC and the leadership of NGOs is neither supported nor supporting.[43] These conditions make the roles and responsibilities for IFO complex and demanding. Accordingly, the CMOC likely will

exercise C2, coordination, or simply information sharing concurrently with the various organizations engaged in IFO.

(11) Figure II-3 presents a conceptual model of the CMOC and the key interfaces intrinsic to IFO. The capabilities required for IFO are independent of the specific structure employed. With the CMOC approach, there is not a "one size fits all" structure appropriate to all areas of operations, scenarios, and missions. The organizational structure and composition is less important than the possession of the capabilities to perform the functions described in the following subsection.

(12) Doctrinally, the CMOC structure is fluid and adaptable to the local conditions and command mission. The CMOC role extends beyond purely financial operations. The JFC already may have a functioning CMOC for conduct of CMO. In those cases, where the roles and responsibilities for the CMOC are established, modification of the existing structure is preferred over creation of a new configuration. However, independent of the membership and organization selected, the CMOC would perform specific IFO tasks. Recent experience in Afghanistan and Iraq indicates that IFO requires:

(a) An integrated civilian–military decision-making structure to set and prioritize objectives in order to create unity of effort and focus stabilization and development efforts down to the local level. A key effort throughout this organizational structure is

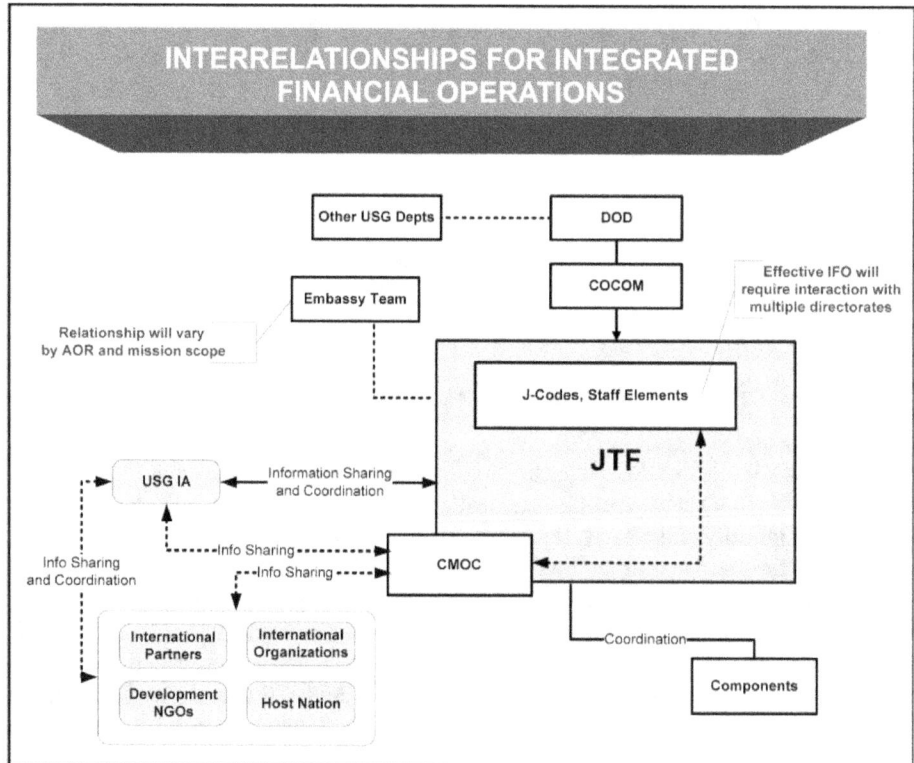

Figure II-3. Interrelationships for Integrated Financial Operations

assessment—are the right things being accomplished to achieve strategic and operational objectives.

(b) A coordination authority responsible for final coordination, provision of civilian-military direction, allocation of resources to USG elements, setting priorities, consulting on priorities with the HN, and working with multinational partners to address common challenges.

(c) A senior working group to make policy and decisions regarding the Civilian-Military Campaign Plan based on input from the national-level working groups, regional civilian-military cells, and the plans and assessment staff.

(d) Processes and procedures for coordination with any regional components engaged in IFO. While their functions would not of necessity be performed with a CMOC, mechanisms must be established for providing support and guidance to subordinate joint force levels, developing and maintaining the integrated civilian-military plan in the region, assessing progress in their region, allocating resources jointly, and raising key issues to engaging with key multinational partners.

(e) A means of assessing IFO activities in the context of achieving strategic and operational objectives. The JFC must be able to determine what the local population expects from the host government, the drivers of instability in the operational area, who or what has the most influence on the perceptions of the local population, and the economic challenges in the operational area.

(f) Establishment of (or if possible utilization of) existing and accepted information sharing and collaboration protocols to work with interagency partners and other external stakeholders engaged in IFO related activities.

(g) Determination of information sharing means in terms of the network, web portals, and email to allow for inclusion of interagency partners, ensuring all parties maintain shared situational awareness and have access to all relevant information.

(h) Development of situational awareness of partner disposition and activities.

(i) Identification and development of any required memorandum of agreement (MOA) to support interagency coordination, command relationships, personnel exchanges, and other important challenges/processes.

(13) The JFC and staff would examine each of these tasks, evaluate these against the command's organizational structure, composition, strategic objectives, IFO partners, staffing, and operational environment; and then would assign specific roles and responsibilities for IFO in the CMOC. These include, but are not limited to planning, KM, CTF, execution monitoring, oversight, and assessment.

c. **Key Advantages**. Adaptation of the CMOC provides a recognizable structure for the planning, execution, and assessment of IFO. Combined with the IFO process, it provides for an IFO coordination and information sharing capability. When completed, the IFO process steps described in Chapter I will contribute to the ability of the JFC to integrate, synchronize, prioritize, and target financial resources and capabilities to achieve desired outcomes. Adoption of this concept has the potential to improve:

(1) **Integration** By providing a locus where the related but incongruent activities of the myriad organizations involved in IFO could be coordinated, organized, or accommodated. A primary benefit is within military, governmental, or IGO hierarchies. The adapted CMOC is the focal point where US military forces could coordinate financial support. The improved integration provided by employment of the process within a CMOC-like context helps to fill key shortfalls in current capabilities, such as the recognized insufficient ability to obtain and maintain situational awareness and transparency of ongoing financial operations, and to understand the multiple funding sources and complex processes when planning financial operations. Doctrinally, the CMOC serves as a platform for engagement and the primary coordination interface for operational and tactical level coordination between the JFC and other stakeholders. This is a principal requirement for conducting effective IFO. A CMOC is formed to receive, validate, and coordinate requests for support from NGOs, IGOs, and regional organizations. The CMOC then forwards these requests to the joint force for action.[44] Hence, the CMOC provides the essential unifying tool for integrating disparate financial activities toward the attainment of operational objectives.

(2) **Synchronization**. More than a purely military effort, IFO seeks to refine processes and procedures to synchronize efforts with USG agencies, multinational partners, IGOs, and NGOs to achieve operational objectives. This synchronization of activities requires a cross-functional staff organization that possesses the skills and experiences to deal with a variety of organizations that have their own agendas and objectives.[45] The CMOC fulfills this role. Arrangement of multiple, concurrent activities in time and space requires unified action. Assignment of IFO synchronization responsibilities to the CMOC supports such an approach. The CMOC, with its standing capability can serve as the JFC's primary coordination interface with other USG agencies, multinational partners, IGOs, and NGOs. As a senior USG official noted, "Possibly the most practical mechanism for ensuring coherence and cooperation is the CMOC. The flexible, situation-specific CMOC may well be the instrument of choice for broad international and other coordination in the field."[46] Total synchronization remains challenging in a purely military operation. The added complexities inherent in IFO, make this an even more difficult and complex task. However, the process steps and tasks are designed to mitigate these difficulties and enable the JFC to optimize synchronization of related activities within the assigned operational area.

(3) **Prioritization**. A CMOC can bridge the gap of the unique characteristics of the member organizations, enabling a common-shared understanding of the operational environment, collaboration, and de-confliction of policy, priorities for execution, and inclusion for cooperative planning. The process requires consideration of the relationship of the projects to joint operation/campaign objectives. This will serve to ensure that those projects with the greatest positive effect on the satisfaction of these goals will get higher precedence. The CMOC could provide full visibility of ongoing projects. Although the JFC's range of influence is variable across the organizations engaged in financial operations, knowledge of ongoing activities could permit more efficient prioritization of projects directly within the JFC's authority.

(4) **Targeting**. JP 3-60, *Joint Targeting*, states "...the purpose of targeting is to integrate and synchronize fires into joint operations. Targeting is the process of selecting and prioritizing targets and matching the appropriate response to them, considering operational requirements and capabilities." In many respects, the use of nonlethal actions, such as IFO, to create desired effects conforms to this description. The same principles for targeting of fires may be adopted for the planning of IFO projects aimed at stabilization and development. Effective targeting of financial resources requires the integration that the CMOC structure can provide. Multiple process steps force consideration of the activities of the other organizations when planning DOD efforts. CTF is an important element in targeting, since the JFC must ensure that the limited funding available is not producing effects that run counter to the attainment of joint operation/campaign objectives. Hence, examination of CTF implications are directed in several IFO process steps and the CMOC structure provides a venue for sharing of CTF related information.

CHAPTER III
ASSESSMENT AND IMPLICATIONS FOR CONDUCTING INTEGRATED FINANCIAL OPERATIONS

UNDERSTANDING POPULACE PRIORITIES

The US Marine Corps' 1st Battalion, 5th Marines, was stationed in the Nawa District, Helmand Province, Afghanistan from April to October of 2009. After security issues were addressed, through the Tactical Conflict Assessment and Planning Framework (TCAPF) surveys, the unit discovered the second most important local grievance was the lack of cell phone coverage. Further TCAPF survey questioning revealed cell phones were the primary and most reliable form of communication for locals to contact their family members who may have been injured in attacks in neighboring areas. Not being able to reach family members created anxiety and a perception of insecurity for the populace. Cell phone towers ranked more important than clinics and jobs, something the unit would not have known without the use of surveys. By establishing cell phone towers, the unit enabled a sense of security among the populace who had the ability to tell others, thus creating support for the unit and the government.

SOURCE: US Agency for International Development (USAID)

1. Introduction

a. Accurate assessment and usable measures of effectiveness (MOE) are vital to successfully integrating financial operations. In order to identify and collect the proper data to support assessment, the clear and concise objectives, outputs, and impact for the proposed activity need to be defined to ensure success and proper measurement.

b. In COIN and stability operations, accurately gauging the effect of money is dependent upon the ability of the JFC to measure the effectiveness or impact of development projects on the local population. To do this the JFC must, in the context of achieving strategic and operational objectives, be able to answer the following questions:

    (1) What does the local population expect from the host government?

    (2) What are the drivers of instability in the operational area?

    (3) Who or what has the most influence on the perceptions of the local population?

    (4) What are the economic challenges in the operational area?

c. JP 2-01-3, *Joint Intelligence Preparation of the Environment*, addresses the need to provide the JFC and staff with necessary information to answer the above questions; while recognizing that stability operations require an approach that places far greater emphasis on understanding the civil population and critical infrastructure.

2. Challenges to Assessment

a. The challenges to assessments must be identified so they can be mitigated, or at least understood if mitigation is not feasible. Without identifying and addressing these challenges, the JFC may draw incorrect conclusions or inferences from existing assessments.

b. **Assessing the cumulative impact of aid or development activities is methodologically challenging.** Gathering this data can be problematic because there are no common data collection or storage procedures among USG agencies, no common language defining the civil-military domain, and no interoperable civil information management system. To mitigate challenges of methodology, assessments may be evaluated by applying the following criteria:

(1) Does an assessment include valid, reliable, and achievable indicators and benchmarks?

(2) Is the assessment data readily available?

(3) Can an assessment even be conducted?

(4) Is there visibility of the project?

Projects should not be implemented if there is no way to track progress or conduct an assessment. Fraud and waste are direct results of improperly managed programs.

c. The following factors are important to all organizations assessing financial operations.

(1) Know the operational area, the people, what they value, and their customs.

(2) Know the history, government, and economic challenges.

(3) Know the root causes of instability.

d. Then, when assessing financial operations, MOEs need to be established that evaluate where the programs and projects are conducted and address those root causes of instability.

e. Intelligence doctrine recognizes that operations which focus on the civil population as a COG require a different mindset and different techniques than a JIPOE effort that focuses on defeating an adversary militarily. IW requires a more detailed understanding of the relevant area's sociocultural factors than is normally the case during traditional war. However, the current intelligence assessment process is primarily focused on adversary courses of action, high value targets, and COGs.

f. **Continuity is a challenge to assessment.** If there is a high personnel turnover rate within operational areas, there is a risk of assessments being changed or a disruption of assessments altogether. While utilization of surveys is a key part of assessing the local population's perceptions, configuration control should be enforced to ensure the same questions are being asked at every interval of the assessment process in order to establish trends. Currently, there is no "central clearinghouse" in Afghanistan for the consolidation and analysis of survey data. There are three nationwide polls by NATO organizations, each separately owned and managed. This begs the question of how much duplication is occurring and how much synergy is lost by not consolidating. Stabilization and development objectives are typically long term, therefore, MOEs and measures of performance (MOPs) should remain consistent and assessments conducted at regular intervals, providing the JFC with valid trend analysis.

3. Implications for Financial Operations

a. Proper assessments are crucial, especially in light of studies that find using financial resources to reconstruct and stabilize an area may not have the intended effects of increasing stability and legitimizing the host government in the eyes of the local populace. British forces deployed a team to Afghanistan, to study the specific security effects of the Employment of Money for Security Effect (MfSyE)- the British military equivalent to MAAWS. Similar to the findings presented herein, this study determined that an absence of visibility and an incomplete understanding of cultural sensitivities leads to poor risk assessment. The findings also acknowledge there is a needed balance of risk between the short-term security effects and long-term stabilization effects. While the British team observed MOEs in place, none directly assessed the effects of the MfSyE projects and lacked the necessary component of monitoring and evaluating over time. The team recommended creating a handbook to not only discuss various funding sources, but also establish an optimal MOE planning cycle. Further, the team suggested implementing training for use of MfSyE funds, as well as conducting a study to determine the level of training needed.

b. The challenge of having proper MOEs in place is reinforced by recent academic critiques of the effectiveness of development aid in support of COIN operations. An accepted component of COIN is the use of aid to separate the population from the insurgency. However, current research based on experiences in Iraq, Afghanistan, and the Philippines question the effectiveness of financial aid in the fight against insurgents. While the research does not refute the need for development assistance, it urges caution in reflexively tying development projects to meeting security objectives, especially those involving large, long-term development projects. There is some evidence that small, community level projects, such as lower magnitude CERP projects that involve the local community in the selection and the execution of the project contribute, at least in the short term, to stability and getting the "foot in the door." Several observations and recommendations emerged from the Wilton Park Conference, "Winning 'Hearts and Minds' in Afghanistan: Assessing the Effectiveness of Development Aid in COIN Operations," held in March 2010:

(1) **Observations**

(a) "Winning hearts and minds" strategies are not evidence-based.

(b) "Peace Penalty" occurs – there is a tendency to spend more money in areas of greater violence leading to perceptions of corruption and favoritism.

(c) Aid creates "transactional" good will, but does little to change the attitude of the population towards the host government or towards foreign military presence.

(d) CERP non-construction projects are more effective than other aid.

(e) Constant interaction with local communities, i.e., projects implemented through a PRT, greatly improves the impact of aid.

(f) Large injects of money that cannot be absorbed by the HN promotes corruption/bad governance leading to increased instability.

(2) **Recommendations**

(a) The COIN strategy needs to be evidence-based.

(b) Concentrate development aid in more secure areas.

(c) Utilize smaller projects that have local participation. Increased visibility leads to improved stability — stabilization is about building trust and relationships.

(d) Project design needs to include pre-, during-, and post-assessment mechanisms to be able to determine the effectiveness of the project.

(e) Sustainability must be a critical factor in the decision on whether or not to implement a project.

(f) Spend less and do it better — only do as much as you can effectively manage and assess.[47]

4. Existing Assessment Tools

a. There are several existing capabilities that can support the JFC in assessment of financial operations. The list below is not intended to be all inclusive nor is the intent to offer an endorsement to any one process or capability. The inclusion of these assessment tools is designed to make the reader aware of the efforts across the interagency community towards effective assessment.

b. The Interagency Conflict Assessment Framework (ICAF) is a tool that enables a team comprised of a variety of USG agency representatives to assess conflict situations systematically and collaboratively, and prepare for interagency planning for conflict prevention, mitigation, and stabilization. It was developed by DOS/CRS, who is the current implementer of this tool in multi-agency situations. The purpose of the ICAF is to develop a commonly held understanding, across relevant USG agencies of the dynamics driving and mitigating violent conflict within a country that informs US policy and planning decisions. It may also include steps to establish a strategic baseline against which USG en-gagement can be evaluated. Importantly, it is a process, and a tool, available for use by any USG agency to supplement interagency planning. An ICAF analysis should be part of the first step in any interagency planning process to inform the establishment of USG goals, design or reshape activities, implement or revise programs, or reallocate resources. This would be included in the mission analysis portion of the JOPP. The interagency planning process within which an ICAF analysis is performed determines who initiates and participates in an ICAF analysis, time and place for conducting it, type of product needed, how the product will be used, and the level of classification required. The operational environment/situation tends to reveal which agencies and individuals should serve on the team and in what capacities they should serve. For example, an established Country Team may use the ICAF analysis to inform Country Assistance Strategy development. Alternatively, USAID and the S/CRS, or a regional bureau, may co-lead an interagency team performing an ICAF analysis in order to assist in developing a NDAA Section 1207 request. Likewise, the State Office of Political/Military Affairs could also conduct an ICAF analysis, or, DOD may lead a team conducting an ICAF analysis to bring an interagency perspective to its theater security cooperation planning.

c. USAID developed Tactical Conflict Assessment and Planning Framework (TCAPF) to provide a simplified framework to identify, target, and prioritize stabilization efforts. This basic collection tool is used to assist individuals in starting conversations with populations. Once initiated, the user is able to explore more in-depth assessments, gaining a fuller understanding of the operational environment. It can serve as a baseline for development aid, but only as a beginning step. The TCAPF process is divided into five steps:

(1) Collect information on the local population's problems/grievances;

(2) Analyze this information, plus other information streams, to identify sources of instability in each operational area;

(3) Design activities to address these sources of instability;

(4) Implement the activities; and

(5) Evaluate the impact of these activities in helping foster stability.

d. The TCAPF provides a common view of sources of instability and provides a prioritization mechanism. Four questions are asked to understand the local population's perspectives:

(1) Has the number of people in the village changed in the last year?

(2) What are the most important problems facing the village?

(3) Who do you believe can solve your problems?

(4) What should be done first to help the village?

Each question is followed with "Why?" The answers to these questions will provide data critical for useful and relevant measures of effectiveness. TCAPF is currently in use among some military units in Afghanistan and is described in Army FM 3-07, *Stability Operations*.

e. The Theater Operational Planning Assessment Service (TOPAS) is a web-enabled strategic and operational capability that supports collaborative planning, decision support, and assessments based on the JOPP. The assessment module is a metrics-based assessment tool, designed in accordance with joint planning and assessment processes, that can track over time the achievement of operational objectives and end states. One of the more interesting capabilities is the ability to create tailored outputs such as PowerPoint briefings to reflect trend analysis or point-in-time assessments. TOPAS is currently an advanced concept and technology demonstration and is, or has been, utilized in Korea and other portions of the Pacific theater, Europe, and Afghanistan. US Army Project Management Battle Command is the technical lead for this capability. It is deployed on both classified and unclassified networks.

f. Surveys are a critical assessment tool in support of COIN operations. When the objectives of the joint operation/campaign span security, governance, and development issues; it is vital to find metrics that reflect the perception of the host country population. Regardless of the successful accomplishment of all ongoing stabilization and development efforts, ultimately, the success of these efforts needs to be measured against the perceptions of the population. Surveys can be utilized to gather data on attitudes, opinions, values, experiences, expectations and needs, and results can be compared over time. It is especially difficult constructing effective surveys for different cultures and in different languages. The challenges to assessment mentioned earlier are especially critical when constructing and administering surveys.

5. Conducting Assessments

The Army Center for Lessons Learned or "CALL" has produced the *Assessment and Measures of Effectiveness in Stability Operations Handbook*. The handbook offers guidance to commanders and their staffs on the fundamentals and purpose of assessments to ensure projects will deliver expected services and effectively legitimize the host government in the eyes of the populace. By understanding the importance of conducting assessments, the commander will allow for "a common operational picture shared by US military and government departments and agencies in the area of operations (AO)."[48] Creating the common operational picture will enable greater visibility, which will lead to better coordination with other participating organizations.

CHAPTER IV
TRAINING REQUIREMENTS

"Members of the Department of Defense shall receive, to the maximum extent possible, timely and effective individual, collective, and staff training, conducted in a safe manner, to enable performance to standard during operations."

DOD Directive 1322.18, Military Training

1. Introduction

a. Training is necessary to ensure proper implementation of IFO. SIGAR Audit-09-01 and GAO Report 09-615, represent reports that address the issue of inadequately trained staff. The aforementioned GAO Report noted that although DOD policy mandates effective and timely training, frequently personnel were not adequately trained prior to deployment.[49] Lack of trained staff is not a result of inadequate training materials available, but due more to a lack of knowledge concerning what is currently available, when training is required.

b. While there is an extensive amount of training for conducting financial operations, as discussed above, it is introduced mostly from a tactical level versus looking at financial operations from a higher, strategic level and how these operations are integrated with operational and strategic planning. Possessing tactical knowledge is crucial for understanding higher implications. However, in order to meet the strategic requirements of IFO, JFCs and their staffs must combine tactical financial operations training with doctrine on joint operations, specifically taking note of the pervasive multi-agency environment. This handbook intends to help bridge the gap between tactical and strategic financial operations, offering insights and best practices on how to best accomplish IFO, given the lack of doctrine concerning IFO.

c. JP 4-10, *Operational Contract Support*, states that personnel serving as contracting officer appointed representatives, such as Field Ordering Officers (FOOs), Government Purchase Card (GPC) holders, or Contracting Officer's Representatives (CORs) require "formal, requisite training in order to serve as ordering officials."[50] Formal training is the desired way to acquire the skills necessary for deployment and ideally should be completed prior to deployment. The Defense Acquisition University and the Army provides this formal training. The USCENTCOM Contracting Command (formerly Joint Contracting Command - Iraq/Afghanistan (JCC-I/A) conducts training in theater for most of the financial operation roles/positions, including CORs and FOOs.

d. This chapter will detail the existing training materials available to joint force staffs and personnel down to the unit level that will be involved in financial operations. The training materials discussed in this chapter are intended as a supplement to formal training and are available whether staff members are preparing to deploy or are already in country. Training materials will be organized by financial operations/roles, interagency environments, assessment training, and IFO-applicable joint doctrine.

2. Handbooks Concerning Financial Operations and Roles

a. Three handbooks address the use of monies in post-conflict environments: the CALL *Commander's Guide to Money as A Weapons System*, USFOR-A's *Money as A Weapons System Afghanistan* (USFOR-A-Pub 1-06), and the Multi-National Corps- Iraq (MNC-I) *Money as A Weapon's System* (MNC-I C8 SOP). These handbooks all cover essentially the same material, with emphasis on certain aspects that are unique to their particular operational area. A preferred sequence is to begin with CALL's guide, which is more general, and then read either of the other two depending on deployment to Afghanistan or Iraq. All provide an overview of the different funds/programs available to the JFC, (operations and maintenance (O&M), military construction (MILCON), CERP, Logistics Civilian Augmentation Program (LOGCAP), military personnel-Army (MPA), other procurement-Army (OPA), and Official Representation Funds (ORF)) detailing acceptable uses and rules governing different monies as well as an outline of the different roles within the implementation of MAAWS and their specific duties. These roles are: FOO, paying agent (PA), project purchasing officer (PPO), contracting officer (KO), COR, contingency contracting officer (CCO), disbursing officer (DO), and the procuring contract officer (PCO). The JFC and applicable staffs, who are responsible for the oversight of CERP funds, are advised to read these handbooks, particularly concentrating on usage of CERP funds.

b. While the three MAAWS handbooks give basic information about the responsibilities of the aforementioned roles, there are a few more detailed handbooks available for certain positions including COR, FOO, and PA.

(1) CORs are responsible for providing oversight of all contract matters including "invoicing and payment, contract changes, contract options, contractor management, property management, contract monitoring, performance reporting, performance remedies, and contract closeout."[51] This is an extremely important function, especially in the monitoring of ongoing projects and proper performance evaluations of contractors. It is critical that CORs are also cognizant of CTF concerns when overseeing ongoing projects. Since CORs are frequently appointed by commanders after the contract award, it is imperative CORs are aware of CALL's *Deployed COR Handbook*, which provides detailed information concerning COR responsibilities.

(2) FOOs and PAs are charged with a ready source of cash and are responsible for dealing with local nationals as they make over-the-counter local purchases. CALL's *Field Ordering Officer and Paying Agent Handbook* serves as a supplement to formal training provided by the supporting contracting office (FOOs) and disbursing office (PAs).[52] CALL's *Unit Commander's Guide to Paying Agents* assists commanders, as well as PAs and FOOs, in understanding and performing their pay duties. In addition to defining roles, responsibilities and procedures, the handbook addresses how money can be used to support the indigenous population in the COIN environment. Additional training for FOOs with emphasis on Afghanistan or Iraq can be found in the *Standard Operating Procedures (SOP) for Field Ordering Officers*.

c. In addition to the MAAWS handbooks, the *Commander's Emergency Response Program Handbook*[53] offers specific guidance on the use of CERP monies. Also produced by CALL, the handbook is a reference for brigade, battalion, and PRT commanders to apply

CERP within their operational area with regard to the legal and regulatory requirements of CERP. The handbook details the approved and unapproved uses of CERP monies as well as accepted principles of reconstruction and development that the commander should consider before undertaking projects.

d. The John Warner NDAA FY07[54] and the NDAA FY08[55] required the DOD to revise and develop new joint policies for contingency contracting and training for personnel outside the acquisition workforce. In response, the DOD created *Contingency Con tracting: A Joint Handbook for the 21st Century* (also referred to as the *Joint Contingency Contracting Handbook)* and the *Joint Contingency Contracting Officer's Representative Handbook.*

(1) The *Joint Contingency Contracting Handbook* includes updated chapters on JP 4-10 and serves as a standardized contingency contracting guide. It is the basis for Defense Acquisitions University's (DAU) Contingency Contracting Course, CON 234. The handbook is issued with a DVD that contains contingency contracting tools, templates, websites, checklists, and standardized training modules.[56]

(2) The *Joint Contingency Contracting Officer's Representative Handbook* is based upon the *Deployed COR Handbook*, mentioned earlier in the chapter. It is supplemented with additional information to serve as a joint resource. With a chapter directed towards commanders on how to choose a COR, the bulk of the handbook is written for the COR, detailing responsibilities and the details of contingency contracting.

e. All CALL handbooks are available through their website and the URL address can be found in Appendix C, "Commander's Guide to Integrated Financial Operations References."

3. Online Training Resources Concerning Financial Operations and Roles

a. In addition to the handbooks, the Defense Acquisition University (DAU) offers a mixture of knowledge sharing assets and continuous learning course (CLC) modules that are available through their website. DAU manages its content through various knowledge portals and repositories such as the Defense Acquisition Portal (DAP), the Acquisition Community Connection (ACC), DOD Acquisition Best Practices Clearinghouse (PBCh), DOD Acquisition Encyclopedia (ACQuipedia), the ACQuire search and discovery system, and the David D. Acker Library and Knowledge Repository. CLC modules can be taken for credit or browsed through for self-refreshing on material. Modules not only focus on specific roles such as those addressing the roles and responsibilities of commanders in the use of contractors, CCO refreshers, and basic skill set of CORs; but also more general courses on contractual incentives, performance- based service acquisitions, and construction contracting. Individuals may search the ACQuire database, a search service of DAU, for various topics concerning the use of monies in post-conflict situations.[57]

b. The *Ask a Professor* feature is a DOD resource for posing questions related to the policies and practices of acquisitions. There is an extensive amount of questions that have already been asked, organized by subject areas. It is strongly encouraged to peruse these subject areas before asking a new question. Questions are answered by personnel of DAU as well as personnel from the Air Force Materiel Command, Assistant Secretary of the Army,

Acquisition, Logistics, & Technology (ASA(ALT)), Defense Contract Audit Agency (DCAA), Defense Institute of Security Assistance Management (DISAM), Defense Security Service (DSS), Information Resources Management College (IRMC), Joint Chiefs of Staff, and Naval Air Systems Command (NAVAIR).[58] The DAU website can be found in Appendix C, References and Additional sources.

c. The Defense Procurement and Acquisition Policy (DPAP) website contains electronic copies of handbooks concerning contingency contracting matters. The *Joint Contingency Contracting Handbook* also resides on the site, serving as an additional online tool, by providing updated information, a portal for sharing tools and templates, and real-time support for contingency contracting staff.[59]

d. The USCENTCOM Contracting Command (formerly JCC-I/A) maintains an online portal providing training and policy documentation, more notably for KOs. There are links and documents pertaining to training of the procurement desktop defense software used by KOs, and SOPs concerning contracting.

e. The US Army Training and Doctrine Command (TRADOC), under the lead-direction of the US Army Financial Management School (USAFMS), has provided CERP functional training through The Army Distributed Learning Program's (TADLP) distributed Learning (dL) component. TADLP plans to offer a web-based, sixteen-hour, dL CERP course that instructs on the various roles, responsibilities, and processes through scenario based exercises. Upon completion, participants will receive a course completion certificate. In the near future, dL will offer a forty-hour module-based CERP training course, which will provide select tracks of training for the different roles/functional areas involved in CERP administration.[60]

4. Handbooks and Online Sources Concerning Unified Action

a. The concept of IFO centers around the proper utilization of monies, ensuring it meets the overarching goal of winning the desired perception from the HN population. While understanding how to distribute and manage funds is one component of IFO, there is also the consideration of how to deal with existing stakeholders in the operational area, who arrive with their own goals, objectives, and funds. In order to adequately address the ability to integrate, synchronize, prioritize, and target fiscal resources and capabilities, military forces on the ground must be able to effectively operate within multi-agency environment.

b. USJFCOM, Joint Warfighting Center (JWFC) has published pamphlets and handbooks addressing post-conflict interagency efforts in a series called the *Unified Action Handbook Series*. Four of these handbooks could prove useful in educating the JFC and staff on the important factors and considerations of working in an operational area that consists of multiple stakeholders.

(1) **Book One**, *Handbook for Military Participation in the Interagency Management System for Reconstruction and Stabilization*, outlines joint force roles and responsibilities in the Interagency Management System (IMS) and existing interagency coordination authorities and mechanisms. It aligns with the *USG Planning Framework for Reconstruction, Stabilization, and Conflict Transformation*. It will also align with the *IMS Guide* under development at the DOS S/CRS.

(2) **Book Two**, *Military Support to Essential Services and Critical Infrastructure*, defines services essential to sustain human life during stability operations (water, sanitation, transportation, medical, etc.), the infrastructure needed to deliver such services, and potential joint force responsibilities.

(3) **Book Three**, *Military Support to Governance, Elections, and Media* provides pre-doctrinal guidance for joint force support to good governance, political competition, and support to media.

(4) **Book Four**, *Military Support to Economic Stabilization* addresses conducting a comprehensive economic assessment, employment and business generation, trade, agriculture, financial sector development and regulation, and legal transformation. These factors are of interest to other stakeholders attempting to rebuild a nation and it is beneficial to understand how the joint forces can support the endeavors.

c. Another handbook of interest is *Interagency Management of Complex Crisis Operations Handbook*, Published by the NDU. This document describes the interagency process and the different coordinating mechanisms in place. It also provides planning and assessment tools which, as discussed previously in Chapter II, is a vital aspect of the JFC's ability to prioritize and target financial resources. While the particular agencies involved in any given operational area will differ, the handbook offers a helpful appendix of USG agencies that have been involved in past operations.

d. USJFCOM's Joint Knowledge Online (JKO) is the Joint Knowledge Development Distribution Capability (JKDDC) for delivering joint train capability through web-based courses and learning tools. For deployed individuals , JKO provides self-paced, pre-deployment training curricula via military NIRPNET, SIPRNET, and public Internet. Courses range from civil military operations to JTF integration, information management, communications, and many more. A course catalog can be found on their website, listed in Appendix C.

5. Joint Doctrine Relevant to Integrated Financial Operations

a. JP 1-06, *Financial Management Support in Joint Operations*, provides doctrine for financial management (FM) in support of joint operations, to include multinational and interagency financial coordination considerations. FM supports accomplishment of the JFC's mission by providing two different, but mutually supporting, core functions: resource management (RM) and finance support. RM includes providing advice and recommendations to the commander; developing command resource requirements; identifying sources of funds; determining costs; acquiring funds; distributing and controlling funds; tracking costs and obligations; capturing costs; establishing reimbursement procedures; and establishing management internal controls. Finance support includes providing financial advice and recommendations; supporting the procurement process; providing limited pay support; and providing disbursing support.

b. JP 3-08, *Interorganizational Coordination During Joint Operations*, addresses the interorganizational environment, core competencies, organizational structures and relationships, potential relationships with the Armed Forces, and how to facilitate coordination with the DOD.

c. JP 3-33, *Joint Task Force Headquarters*, provides joint doctrine on the formation and employment of a joint task force (JTF) HQ to command and control joint operations. It introduces the JTF concept and provides details on organization and staffing, C2, intelligence, operations, logistics, plans and policy, and communications system support. The JTF may apply various organization, staffing, and command relationships based on the mission and operational environment, and to accommodate operations with interagency, multinational, IGO, and NGO partners. It acknowledges the focal point for operational and tactical level coordination with civilian agencies may occur at the JTF HQ, the civil-military operations center (CMOC), or the humanitarian operations center.

d. JP 3-57, *Civil Military Operations*, contains joint doctrine on the planning and conduct of CMO by joint forces, the use of civil affairs forces, and the coordination with other capabilities contributing to the execution of CMO to achieve unity of effort. The purpose of CMO is to serve as a primary military instrument to synchronize military and nonmilitary instruments of national power, particularly in support of stability, COIN, and other operations to oppose "asymmetric" and "irregular" threats. The JFC must ensure the CMO is coordinated not only at the operational level, but also at the country and theater strategic levels.

e. JP 4-10, *Operational Contract Support*, establishes doctrine for planning, conducting, and assessing operational contract support integration and contractor management functions in support of joint operations. It provides standardized guidance and information related to integrating operational contract support and contractor management, defines and describes these two different, but directly related functions, and provides a basic discussion on contracting C2 organizational options. It does not pertain to DOD contracting support of routine, recurring (i.e., noncontingency) operations. It also does not provide a significant discussion of construction-related contracting since this topic is covered in depth by JP 3-34, *Engineering Operations*. Commanders and their staffs must have a working knowledge of key joint contract support integration and contractor management related terms, since these terms are not widely known outside of the professional acquisition community.

f. JP 5-0, *Joint Operation Planning*, provides current doctrine concerning conducting joint, interagency, and multinational planning activities across the range of military operations using adaptive planning — "the joint capability to create and revise plans rapidly and systematically, as circumstances require." Joint operation planning encompasses the mobilization, deployment, employment, and sustainment of forces. JFCs and staffs are encouraged to coordinate and integrate with civilian agencies, early on in the planning process. To facilitate planning, the JOPP is introduced as seven logical steps to analyze a mission and to develop, analyze, and compare alternate COAs.

6. Integrated Financial Operations Training

The NDU is currently proposing IFO inputs to its curriculum and will use this handbook for existing classes. The College of International Security Affairs (CISA) and the Industrial College of the Armed Forces (ICAF) also are proposing to circulate guides to its faculty for inclusion in existing courses.

7. Additional Research and Study

a. **Research and Study**. IFO covers a wide range of activities that are beyond the scope of this handbook and there are several areas that require additional research and study. Some of these are discussed below.

b. Examination of a KM application or software solution to provide visibility and enable coordination across military and civilian organizations to effectively implement IFO. Gaining and maintaining situational awareness of all current and planned projects within the operational area is a challenge. This includes examining existing capabilities and emerging technologies to see if they can be easily modified or adapted to meet the requirements of IFO. One of the options seen as most promising is the All Partners Access Network" or "APAN." This capability was utilized by US Southern Command during the relief efforts following the Haiti Earthquake. It enabled net-centric sharing of information supporting the operation among USG agencies and UN relief organizations. It included the ability for both unstructured (wikis, blogs) and structured (databases, geospatial data) collaboration. This is currently the enterprise solution for two major Joint Concept Technology Demonstrations (JCTD), i.e., Cooperative Security and Joint Civil Information Management. Both JCTDs involve multiple USG agencies.

c. This handbook focuses on the JTF level of implementation and the management of only a portion of in-theater DOD funds. Other sources, such as dollars coming in from CONUS commands, security assistance spending, and the impact of military support spending, e.g., FOB construction, on local populations were not studied. Understanding the impact of these funding lines and incorporating their effects will play an important factor in implementing a comprehensive IFO strategy.

d. The effectiveness of development/stability spending on achieving COIN objectives is not well understood; however, as described in Chapter III, "Assessment and Implications for Conducting Integrated Financial Operations," extensive research is now being conducted in this area. Further study in this area would give the JFC a better understanding of how the expenditure of funds in these areas affects mission accomplishment.

e. Creating an effective intergovernmental working group is a key component of IFO; however, the principles outlined for the CMOC organizational construct are high level and require additional detail to operationalize. Examining the various leadership and management strategies under different operational conditions would provide valuable insights to future JFC executing IFO.

f. The linkages between anti-corruption and antiterrorism efforts and IFO have not been thoroughly examined. The diverse nature and makeup of the IFO COI make the conduct of these activities in an operational environment challenging.

Additional information for further study is available on USJFCOM's JKO and the Joint Doctrine, Education, and Training Electronic Information System (or JDEIS)

8. Conclusion

There are various resources available to help train and educate military forces in financial operations, contracting, and multi-agency environments. By having adequate knowledge in these subject areas, and ensuring the joint force staff possesses adequate knowledge, the JFC will be able to effectively conduct and implement planning, execution, and assessment for IFO into the overall joint operation/campaign plan. All resources mentioned in this chapter are fully listed in Appendix C, "Commander's Guide to Integrated Financial Operations References."

CHAPTER V
OPERATIONAL IMPLICATIONS

1. General

a. Improved command emphasis on financial operations has brought about some degree of success; however, effective IFO are hampered by community stovepipes, immature policy, insufficient doctrine, and inadequate training. Full and effective implementation of IFO requires adoption of doctrine, organization, training, materiel, leadership and education, personnel, and facilities (DOTMLPF) solutions. Continuing implementation and evaluation of IFO should consider the consequences across the DOTMLPF spectrum.

b. More work needs to be done to identify an end state for IFO within DOD, analyze existing doctrinal processes to determine needed modification, and provide organizational constructs to support the process changes. Investigating and implementing ways to reach out and coordinate IFO activities with multinational and non-military partners will provide significantly improved coherence and unity of effort towards achieving the joint operation/campaign objectives. This guide is the first attempt to map the IFO process and to propose an existing organizational construct, i.e., the CMOC, to accomplish the required coordination necessary for effective IFO.

c. To better facilitate implementation of IFO, the joint community needs to incorporate the IFO process, as described in Chapter II, into joint doctrine. This effort should include defining the scope and limitations of IFO, identifying value-added organizational changes and practices, and supporting capabilities and relationships. Training and education may be the key enabler to rapidly increase the effectiveness of IFO and facilitate the adoption of more effective organizational methods. Training staff members to better synchronize financial operations with other joint operations can help the JFC more effectively utilize financial operations to achieve joint operation/campaign objectives.

2. Doctrine

a. JP 1-06, *Financial Management Support in Joint Operations*, provides guidance to JFCs and staffs for the management of financial resources. However, the focus of JP 1-06 is to provide mission-essential funding and reduce the impact of insufficient funding on joint force readiness. It is not designed to address planning, coordinating, executing, and assessing financial operations by various military and non-military organizations to support the achievement of operational objectives.

b. Considerations for further development or revision of joint doctrine include the following:

(1) A more thorough discussion of IFO employment in pertinent joint operations and functions including the JOPP as described in JPs 3-0, *Joint Operations* and 5-0, *Joint Operation Planning*, is needed. This discussion could include an IFO vignette and considerations for making IFO a main effort during certain phases of a joint operation/campaign. These keystone documents should address the growing importance of the role of IFO in IW, COIN, and stability operations. The IFO functions also are pertinent to

three of the four military activities (i.e., security, engagement, relief and reconstruction) defined in the *Capstone Concept for Joint Operations* (Version 3.0). Identification of financial operations challenges that are unique to the various types of military operations should help planners adapt to emerging circumstances more quickly.

(2) Extensive discussions of interorganizational coordination are included in JPs 3-08, *Interorganizational Coordination During Joint Operations*, 3-33, *Joint Task Force Headquarters*, 3-57 *Civil Military Operations* and 3-24, *Counterinsurgency Operations*, including a discussion of organizational approaches. These discussions also should highlight the importance of unified action when conducting financial operations in the operational area. The discussion should address processes and organizational approaches that will create opportunities to fully integrate all financial operations into the accomplishment of joint operation/campaign objectives. An agreed upon list of areas for coordination, coupled with the IFO process, should improve the speed and focus of efforts among military and non-military organizations.

(3) Identification and incorporation of compatible assessment techniques and procedures utilized by the various agencies and organizations involved in financial operations will benefit assessment planning. Assessment needs to be addressed in virtually all of the above mentioned joint publications. Preparation for and assessment of long term operations such as financial operations also needs to be addressed in JPs 2-01, *Joint and National Intelligence Support to Military Operations*, and 2-01.3, *Joint Intelligence Preparation of the Operational Environment*.

(4) The importance, complexity, and breadth of IFO may validate the need for a new joint publication on IFO. This handbook could provide the core content.

b. The primary joint publications that likely need a discussion of IFO include:

(1) JP 1, *Doctrine for the Armed Forces of the United States*,

(2) JP 1-06, *Financial Management Support in Joint Operations*,

(3) JP 2-01, *Joint and National Intelligence Support to Military Operations*,

(4) JP 2-01.3, *Joint Intelligence Preparation of the Operational Environment*,

(5) JP 3-0, *Joint Operations*,

(6) JP 3-08, *Interorganizational Coordination During Joint Operations*,

(7) JP 3-24, *Counterinsurgency Operations*,

(8) JP 3-33, *Joint Task Force Headquarters*,

(9) JP 3-57, *Civil Military Operations*, and

(10) JP 5-0, *Joint Operation Planning*.

3. Organization

a. When a new concept is introduced there is a natural tendency to jump to an organizational solution before fully understanding the process adjustments that are required. A complete understanding of the detailed procedures required to execute IFO is required prior to allocation of more resources and or implementation of organizational change.

b. Whether or not organizational changes are necessary, those leaders responsible for implementing, coordinating, or directing IFO activities for their command must be given the requisite authority and tools to accompany the responsibility. Diminishing stovepipes among reviewing authorities that restrain the effective employment of financial resources is critical to the success of IFO. While this may require revision of staff processes and procedures within joint organizations, the results should be a single coherent effort that can more effectively meet the challenge of conducting successful operations at all levels.

c. This handbook has recommended the CMOC as an appropriate organizational construct to meet the requirements for coordination among all parties conducting IFO. The intent is not to be directive but to identify an organization with doctrinal underpinnings that provides the ability to coordinate, and synchronize financial operations in time and space, and to prioritize and target limited financial resources toward the achievement of joint operation/ campaign objectives.

4. Training

a. Joint exercises with interagency participation in IFO scenario events that prompt planning and coordination interaction would provide a significant benefit. Interagency partner participation will provide the JFC and his staff greater visibility of the non-DOD capabilities that can be employed. Evaluation of the IFO process and holistic approach to IFO during joint exercises and experiments would be beneficial. Near-term opportunities include USJFCOM J7 controlled venues such as Joint Knowledge Online (JKO) courses and Mission Rehearsal Exercises (MRXs).

b. A multi-pronged approach to integrating IFO into necessary training venues is required to maximize the chance for transition success. Some transition will result from joint doctrine updates. Socialization of this handbook with Service and joint education institutions will result in some curricula change that will evolve from extraction of IFO information to update current courses. Also, the posting of relevant IFO information on the Joint Doctrine, Education, and Training Electronic Information System will promote integration into educational venues.

c. Incorporation of IFO into functional training (e.g., financial management, operational planning, intelligence operations) in the Service schools normally requires staffing through the Joint Capabilities Integration and Development System (JCIDS)/Joint Capabilities Roadmap (JCR). While this may take 18-24 months, this is a critical pathway to more fully integrate IFO into the JOPP.

d. As IFO is more fully integrated into joint operation/campaign plans, there needs to be more time and effort expended to prepare individuals for conducting progress assessments.

Assessment of construction and humanitarian assistance projects goes far beyond tactical assessments such as combat assessment. JP 5-0 emphasizes that continuous assessment is required to determine if the JFC is "doing the right things" and, "As a general rule, the level at which a specific operation, task, or action is directed should be the level at which such activity is assessed." The creation of effective data collection plans is an integral part of planning. To effectively determine the MOEs and how data should be collected requires training at all levels. Research conducted for this handbook indicates that training in support of assessment, especially at the operational and strategic levels, needs to receive greater emphasis.

5. Materiel

a. Research and discussions during the development of this handbook indicate a requirement for a common knowledge management capability so that all organizations planning and conducting financial operations could input and access data to provide a relevant common operational picture of financial operations. This level of visibility and coordination is required in order to conduct "sanity checks" regarding the effectiveness of a project and to insure that projects are not duplicative and indeed support the joint operation/campaign objectives. This capability would contribute directly to the overall effectiveness of IFO.

b. Current challenges to arriving at an effective materiel solution are as follows:

(1) It requires a common network that all military and non-military partners can access. It also must provide adequate security for the protection of project information and individuals executing the projects.

(2) Many individual databases currently exist to support ongoing projects for individual organizations. To combine the data will require the ability to move large amounts of data among disparate databases into one overarching database.

(3) Continuous cooperation by all participants to maintain the currency of the database, and a willingness to collaborate regarding duplication or the effectiveness of projects is necessary.

6. Leadership and Education

a. The application of IFO-related capability, planning, and coordination needs to become an integral part of joint professional military education (JPME) and Service education programs including the Capstone, Keystone and Pinnacle programs. This education should include planning considerations for early IFO efforts. Our military leadership, given the current global environment, may significantly benefit from education that provides them with the knowledge necessary to analyze how to better utilize financial operations as an integral part of ongoing military efforts.

b. The creation of a dedicated IFO educational curriculum is in its infancy stage. Currently, the National Defense University staff has agreed to non-resourced injects into the Chief Financial Officer Academy and into the curriculum of some electives that focus on stability and reconstruction at the Industrial College of the Armed Forces.

c. Fully resourced inclusion in the NDU curriculum and JPME II will require more formalized staffing. Proposed curricula changes to JPME flow through the Joint Faculty Education Council and the Military Education Coordination Council. Working with the USJFCOM J7, a proposal for consideration by the JFEC will be drafted for the next submission date.

7. Personnel

The impact on personnel is unknown at this time.

8. Facilities

The impact on facilities is unknown at this time.

9. Conclusion

IFO are a necessary and critical capability in support of COIN and stability operations. IFO also should be fully integrated into pertinent joint operation functions and processes at the outset. Synchronization of IFO throughout joint operation planning, preparation, execution and assessment ensures the greatest effect toward the achievement of joint operation/campaign objectives. Effectively employed IFO potentially can help achieve national- and operational-level objectives and pre-empt the requirement for combat operations. As demonstrated in the research accomplished for this handbook, a more integrated, synchronized, and comprehensive effort is required. A review of all financial operations related processes and capabilities within the USG, with a clearly articulated IFO end state in mind, should serve to guide future DOTMLPF changes that produce an effective IFO solution set.

Intentionally Blank

APPENDIX A
ORGANIZATIONS IN THE OPERATIONAL AREA

1. United States Government Agencies

DEPARTMENT OF DEFENSE	
Organization description/ Programs	DOD is charged with coordinating and supervising all agencies and functions for the USG relating directly to national security and the United States armed forces. The organization and functions of the DOD are set forth in Title 10 of the United States Code (USC). The DOD contributes troops and support for the International Security Assistance Force, under NATO leadership, and provides provincial reconstruction and stabilization efforts to help set the economic, political and security conditions for the growth of an effective, democratic national government in Afghanistan. The US contributes troops to both the ISAF mission and Operation ENDURING FREEDOM, tasked with pursuing al-Qaeda throughout Afghanistan's inhospitable border region with Pakistan.
Relevant Regulation	Title 10 USC; NDAA/; Defense Appropriations
Guidance/ Oversight	President as commander-in-chief; Secretary of Defense (SecDef); combatant commanders who command all military forces in the operational area; SIGAR
Funding	DOD - Operations and Maintenance Funding (O&M) DOD - Afghan Security Forces Fund (ASFF) DOD - CERP DOD - MILCON
Web address	http://www.defense.gov/
UNITED STATES CENTRAL COMMAND	
Organization description/ Programs	US combatant command, along with national and international partners, applies unified action to promote cooperation among nations, respond to crises, deter or defeat state and non-state aggression, support development, and, when necessary, reconstruction in order to establish the conditions for regional security, stability, and prosperity. Oversees the US efforts in Afghanistan and Iraq, and the theater-wide campaign against al-Qaeda. Using the Civil-Military Campaign Plan, the goals in Afghanistan are to disrupt, dismantle, and defeat al-Qaeda and its allies, and enable conditions in Afghanistan for the establishment of legitimate Afghan governance in the eyes of the Afghan people.
Relevant Regulation	• NDAA; Defense Appropriations • *USG Integrated Civilian- Military Campaign Plan for Support to Afghanistan*
Guidance/ Oversight	SecDef; SIGAR
Funding	DOD - ASFF DOD - CERP DOD – MILCON
Web address	www.centcom.mil

DEFENSE SECURITY COOPERATION AGENCY (DSCA)	
Organization description/ Programs	DSCA's Mission is to lead, direct and manage security cooperation programs and resources to support national security objectives that: build relationships that promote US interests; build allied and partner capacities for self-defense and coalition operations in the global war on terrorism; and promote peacetime and contingency access for US forces. DSCA manages security assistance programs that include Foreign Military Sales (FMS), Foreign Military Financing (FMF) grants or loans, and International Military Education and Training (IMET).
Relevant Regulation	Afghanistan Freedom Support Act (AFSA); State Foreign Operations Appropriations FY 2010; DSCA has the authority under the Economy Act (31 USC. § 1535) for financial execution of ASFF-funded orders through the FMS Trust Fund and associated accounting systems.
Guidance/ Oversight	DSCA manages security assistance programs US Department of Defense (DOD) or commercial contractors provide defense articles and services in support of national policies and objectives.
Funding	State Foreign Operations Appropriations for FMF, FMS, IMET. Funds appropriated to the Department of State and authorized under the Foreign Assistance Act are transferred to DSCA for execution.
Web address	http://www.acq.osd.mil/dpap/cpic/ic/afghanistan.html
NATIONAL GUARD / AGRIBUSINESS DEVELOPMENT TEAM	
Organization description/ Programs	The National Guard's Agribusiness Development Teams are designed to promote sustainable farming practices in Afghanistan, a country in which 85% of the population makes a living from agriculture. Projects include training, equipping and facilitating agricultural services via infrastructure development.
Relevant Regulation	NDAA, State Foreign Operations Appropriations, USDA
Guidance/ Oversight	Organized and deployed under the DOD/National Guard, ADT's partner work with the PRTs and the DOA, USAID, US land grant colleges and universities, the Afghan national and provincial governments, Afghan farmers and agriculture businesses, and NGOs.
Funding	No dedicated Funds. Uses Commanders Emergency Response Funds (CERP); or partner resources from USDA or USAID
Web address	http://www.ng.mil/features/ADT/default.aspx
US AIR FORCE CENTER FOR ENGINEERING AND THE ENVIRONMENT	
Organization description / Programs	Provides integrated engineering and environmental management, execution, and technical services that optimize US Air Force (USAF) and joint capabilities through sustainable installations. Fourteen on-going contingency construction projects under the Combined Security Transition Command- Afghanistan provide construction of facilities for military headquarters, training, education, airfields, logistics, police stations, etc; and provisions for architecture and engineering services.
Relevant Regulation	NDAA
Guidance/ Oversight	DOD/USAF coordination with USFOR-A; DOS, US Emb Kabul and ISAF.
Funding	DOD Afghanistan Supplemental
Web address	http://www.afcee.af.mil

US FORCES AFGHANISTAN	
Organization description/ Programs	A headquarters intended to enable the most efficient C2 of USFOR-A and ensure effective integration and coordination between US and coalition forces operating under NATO/ISAF.
Relevant Regulation	NDAA
Guidance/ Oversight	DOD
Funding	DOD/ Afghanistan Supplemental/ Operations Funds. For 2009 the USFOR-A budget equaled $60 billion, of which 95% was spent on combat operations and 5%, or $3 billion, on development-related activities. Since US forces began operating in Afghanistan in 2001, total expenditures of USFOR-A are $228.2 billion dollars, with $11 billion being spent on non-combat or development-related activities.
Web address	http://www.nationalpriorities.org/newsletter/2009/12/01/Afghanistan-fact-sheet-numbers-behind-troop-increase
AFGHAN THREAT FINANCE CELL	
Organization description/ Programs	Operational in mid 2009 (scheduled to be fully operational in 2010), ATFC is a fusion center headed by the DEA with TREAS and DOD as co-deputies. Located at Bagram Air Base, it is a multi-agency organization that includes thirty specialists from the DEA, TREAS, DOJ, USCENTCOM, CIA, and FBI. ATFC is responsible for the development, coordination, and execution of combatant command and interagency actions that identify and prioritize financial operations, facilities, or personalities whose efforts significantly influence the operations, direction, or funding of terrorists and consequent insurgencies throughout the GCC's AOR. Using a multi-pronged approach, the ATFC scrutinizes the hawala networks, an informal banking system popular with the Taliban for moving monies quickly and cheaply. ATFC works with Afghanistan's domestic intelligence agency, the Afghan National Directorate for Security's Major Crimes Task Force, the Anti-Corruption Unit for prosecution, and the Anti-Corruption Tribunal (part of the Afghan Supreme Court).
Relevant Regulation	
Guidance/ Oversight	• Headed by the DEA • US TREAS liaison to the ATFC
Funding	DEA, DOD
Web address	http://armedservices.house.gov/pdfs/TUTC031109/Fridovich_Testimony031109.pdf http://www.america.gov/st/texttrans-english/2010/January/20100128150308eaifas0.2595026.html&distid=ucs http://www.globalpost.com/dispatch/afghanistan/100119/afghanistan-corruption-us-investigation

USCENTCOM CONTRACTING COMMAND (FORMERLY JOINT CONTRACTING COMMAND IRAQ/AFGHANISTAN [JCC-I/A])	
Organization description/ Programs	USCENTCOM Contracting Command (aka Joint Theater Support Contracting Command [JTSCC]), a major subordinate provisional command of USCENTCOM, provides contracting support to military forces to obtain vital supplies and services not available through logistics capabilities. JCC-I/A was created to be the one coordinated contracting effort for the operational area. The JCC-I/A Commander works with the Chiefs of Mission (ambassadors of Iraq and Afghanistan), MNF-I, NATO ISAF, and Combined Joint Task Force 82 Afghanistan in a manner that supports the direct mission of operational coalition forces in the relief and reconstruction of Iraq and Afghanistan, and drives capacity building and economic self sufficiency within Iraq and Afghan Ministries in order to build and sustain self-sufficient security forces and help promote economic self-sufficiency within Iraq and Afghanistan. JCC-I/A is authorized to contract for-other-than-military construction and CERP. • Regional contracting center (RCC) - tactical implementers of JCC-I/A operational plan with the mission to provide contingency contracting support for coalition forces, ANA, ANP, and Afghanistan relief/construction efforts. • Senior Contracting Official - Afghanistan (SCO-A) supports contracts for reconstruction and support to military forces. • Works with the Deputy Under SecDef for Business Transformation, USCENTCOM, and the Deputy Assistant Secretary of the Army for Plans and Programs to implement contingency contracting tools. • Supports Afghan Security Forces Funding (ASFF) programs. • Works with Defense Contracting Management Agency (DCMA) who closes out contracts and ensures contractors uphold the contract agreement. • Afghan First Program- procurement preferences for local national businesses. • Portal for US military contracting where Afghan companies are required to register.
Relevant Regulation	• 2004 Central Command Fragmentary Order (FRAGO). • Federal Acquisition Regulation (FAR). • Defense Federal Acquisition Regulation Supplement (DFARS), Procedures, Guidance and Information (PGI). • Army Federal Acquisition Regulation Supplement (AFARS) 5101.304 • JCC-I/A Acquisition Instruction (January 2010).
Guidance/ Oversight	• JCC-I/A provides policy and guidance to acquisition professionals in the operational area. • All management of reconstruction efforts falls under the DOS.
Funding	DOD funding primarily from Additional (Title IX) and Supplemental appropriations- the Joint Theater Contracting Support (JTCS) under the Deputy Assistant Secretary of the Army for Procurement (DASA(P)) ensures JCC-I/ is fully funded.
Web addresses	http://www.dcma.mil/communicator/summer06/3 customer focus/ DCMA Comm v06n03 pp24-pp29.pdf http://hsgac.senate.gov/public/index.cfm?FuseAction Files.View& FileStore id a2b9ba40-9b6c-4171-8348-71809163a239

DEPARTMENT OF STATE	
Organization Description /Programs	The Secretary of State (SECSTATE) coordinates and leads integrated USG efforts, involving all US departments and agencies with relevant capabilities, to prepare, plan, and conduct reconstruction and stabilization activities. When directed by the SECSTATE, S/CRS will coordinate interagency assessment and planning for integrated USG reconstruction and stabilization efforts. Activation of the Interagency Management System (IMS) enables an Interagency Policy Committee (IPC) or the Country Reconstruction and Stabilization Group (CRSG) to accomplish this. If not, the COM and State Department Regional Assistant Secretary or Bureau of Political Military Affairs will lead interagency assessment and planning. In the case of Afghanistan, the DOS provides US foreign policy direction for Afghanistan and resources and expertise to Afghanistan in a variety of areas, including humanitarian relief and assistance, capacity-building, security needs, counter-narcotic programs, and infrastructure projects. • President's Representative in Afghanistan is the Ambassador who reports back through SECSTATE. Counterpart to CMD. • DOS Special Representative for Afghanistan and Pakistan, is responsible for US policy, integration and coordination. • Programs implemented in country under direction of US Ambassador, US Embassy Kabul. At US EMB Kabul, the **Coordinating Director for Development and Economic Affairs,** oversees all US government non-military assistance to Afghanistan. Economic, development, health, refugee assistance, security and law enforcement assistance programs are carried out directly by State Department personnel and indirectly through transfers of DOS funds to other agencies / contractors for execution.
Relevant Regulation	Foreign Assistance Act, as amended; State Foreign Operations Appropriations; Afghanistan Freedom Support Act.
Guidance /Oversight	SECSTATE; US Ambassador; Special Representative for Afghanistan and Pakistan; SIGAR
Funding	State Foreign Operations Appropriations Accounts include: • ESF • Development Assistance (DA) • Child Survival and Health (CSH) • Migration & Refugee Asst. (MRA) • Nonproliferation, Anti-terrorism and Demining (NADR) • International Narcotics and Law Enforcement (INCLE) • Foreign Military Financing (FMF) (executed by DSCA) • International Military Education and Training (IMET)
Web address	http://www.state.gov/p/sca/ci/af/index.htm

US AGENCY FOR INTERNATIONAL DEVELOPMENT	
Organization Description/ Programs	USAID is an independent government agency that receives overall foreign policy guidance from the SECSTATE. USAID advances US foreign policy objectives by supporting economic growth, agriculture and trade, global health and democracy, conflict prevention and humanitarian assistance. USAID has Foreign Service Officers (FSO) posted in US Embassies throughout the world and prepare country assessments. The USAID mission will also be able to provide an overview of foreign and international assistance programs. The USAID Office of Military Affairs also has liaison officers at each GCC who serve as development advisors. In the immediate post-conflict/crisis, USAID Office of US Foreign Disaster Assistance (OFDA) deploys Disaster Assistance Response Teams (DART) that provide immediate "on the ground" assessment, and work routinely with other aid organizations. At the strategic level, coordination with USAID is through the OSD and the Joint Staff (JS) using the IMS, or more routine NSC processes. At the operational and tactical level, coordination is through the geographic combatant commanders (GCC) liaison and Office of Defense Cooperation or Military Groups in the country team. In Afghanistan, USAID's stated strategy is to improve economic growth, democratic governance, health care and education for Afghans. USAID work in Afghanistan is carried out under the USAID Mission which is in the US EMB Kabul. USAID works through implementing partners to provide programs and assistance. USAID personnel work at all levels of government. They support RCs Provincial Reconstruction Teams, Company Commanders and others to provide development guidance. USAID program funds are implemented through contractors, grantees and non-governmental organizations (NGOs). Since 2001, USAID has spent an estimated $7.9 billion in Afghanistan. Programs: • Economic Growth-- Reliable infrastructure, energy networks, power generation, communications, roads, rural economic support, investment markets • Health and Education • Governing Justly and Democratically- Rule of Law, Local Governance and Community Development Programs • Agricultural Development • Humanitarian Assistance
Relevant Regulation	Foreign Assistance Act; Afghanistan Freedom Support Act
Guidance/ Oversight	USAID Administrator; USAID Mission in Afghanistan; State Department Special Representative for Afghanistan/Pakistan; SIGAR
Funding	State Foreign Operations Appropriations • Development Assistance • ESF
Web address	http://afghanistan.usaid.gov//en/Index.aspx

US EMBASSY KABUL	
Organization Description /Programs	The American Embassy (AMEMB) Country Team and its economic section is one of the most important sources of reliable information and analysis. In addition to a State Department economic officer, many embassies have an USAID mission responsible for managing US development assistance programs. Many embassies also have a Department of Commerce Foreign Commercial Service office staffed with personnel who are familiar with commercial conditions and with US trade and investment; and some embassies have an agricultural affairs section staffed by the Department of Agriculture personnel. A complete listing of AMEMB contacts for economic, commercial, agricultural, and USAID assistance programs in each country is under "key officers" on the State Department website.
	US Embassy Kabul is led by the US Ambassador to Afghanistan, the President's Representative in country. The Embassy oversees/coordinates all USG Agencies in country, provides leadership and direction to all USG programs implemented in country, is the civilian counterpart to the military commander in country, and provides liaison to the HN and other donor nations.
	The Embassy oversees DOS, USAID, DOC, DOJ, DHHS, USDA and all other USG civilian agencies in country. It is the contact point to international partners and organizations in Afghanistan. The Embassy also supports small grant projects for outreach; democracy/rule of law.
Relevant Regulation	Foreign Assistance Act, 1961 as Amended; State Foreign Operations Appropriations
Guidance /Oversight	Ambassador; SECSTATE; Assistance Coordinator; SIGAR
Funding	State Foreign Operations Appropriations
Web Address	www.state.gov http://kabul.usembassy.gov

US DEPARTMENT OF COMMERCE	
Organization Description /Programs	The Department of Commerce promotes US trade and investment, strengthens US industry and supports fair trade. The Department of Commerce has an Office of Reconstruction and Stabilization that can coordinate extensive capabilities throughout the various Agencies and Bureaus. In addition to the Foreign Commercial Service global network of trade professionals, it has regional bureaus and offices that possess detailed knowledge of local conditions and actors. In Afghanistan, the DOC works with the US Embassy in Kabul, USAID and others to support economic development.
	Through the DOC, the Afghanistan Investment and Reconstruction Task Force which provides information and counseling to private sector companies interested in business opportunities to expand trade and investment in Afghanistan. Holds Business Development conferences; links US companies to Afghanistan market, identifies trade opportunities.
	http://trade.gov/afghanistan/doc_afghanistan_aboutus.asp

Relevant Regulation	Foreign Assistance Act, DOC Appropriations; State Foreign Operations Appropriations
Guidance/Oversight	Secretary of Commerce, SECSTATE, US Embassy Kabul
Funding	DOC Appropriations; FY 2010 State Foreign Operations Appropriations
Web Address	http://www.commerce.gov

US DEPARTMENT OF HEALTH AND HUMAN SERVICES	
Organization Description /Programs	The DHHS is involved in several activities within Afghanistan. These relate to numerous health areas including hospital training for healthcare professionals, production and distribution of health education materials, provision of safe water, and the mitigation of vaccine-preventable diseases. The DHHS engages the Afghanistan Ministry of Public Health (MOPH) to help implement its National Health Strategy under the internationally monitored Afghanistan National Development Strategy to build sustainable capacity for public health and medical investments. The DHHS carries out direct HHS programs and supports programs of DOS and USAID. **DHHS - Office of Global Health Affairs - Afghanistan Health Initiative (AHI):** Included in the FY 2010 Budget is $6 million to continue support of the DHHS health care initiatives in Afghanistan, particularly in the areas of improving the quality of maternal and neo-natal health care for Afghan mothers and their babies.
Relevant Regulation	Foreign Assistance Act, as Amended
Guidance/Oversight	Secretary HHS, US EMB Kabul
Funding	HHS Appropriations; State Foreign Operations Appropriations via DOS and/or USAID funding transfers.
Web Address	http://www.hhs.gov/

US DEPARTMENT OF JUSTICE	
Organization Description /Programs	Led by the Attorney General, DOJ is comprised of 40 components and enforces federal criminal and civil laws. DOJ is involved in multiple operations and assistance efforts in Afghanistan. Through reimbursable and non-reimbursable details of personnel DOJ provides federal prosecutors, law enforcement agents and other experts to serve as advisors and liaisons to the Government of Afghanistan. DOJ also works with US interagency partners and international partners to develop the judicial and law enforcement sectors in Afghanistan.

Organization Description /Programs	DOJ support includes: • US Attorney's Office (USAO) • DEA • Federal Bureau of Investigation (FBI), • Bureau of Alcohol, Tobacco and Firearms (ATF) • US Marshalls Service (USMS) • National Drug Intelligence Center DOJ supports: • Criminal Justice Task Force (CJTF) at US EMB Kabul. • DEA Foreign Deployed Advisory Support Teams (FAST), which help build infrastructure and establish counter-narcotic capabilities. DEA has provided classroom training for Afghan officials assigned to the National Interdiction Unit and the Counter Narcotics Police of Afghanistan, as well as for British coalition forces. • International Criminal Investigative Training and Assistance Program (ICITAP) funded by DOS, USAID, DOD. • Overseas Prosecutorial Development Assistance and Training Program (OPDAT) –funded by DOS/INL • Efforts of the DOS Coordinator for Reconstruction and Stabilization to build capacity and support development of the "Civilian Response Corps".
Relevant Regulation	Foreign Assistance Act, as amended;
Guidance/Oversight	US Attorney General, US AMB EMB Kabul, SIGAR
Funding	DOJ Appropriations, State Foreign Operations Appropriations; DOS / INL; USAID, and DOD funds CN
Web address	http://www.justice.gov/

US DEPARTMENT OF TREASURY	
Organization Description /Programs	The TREAS, led by the Secretary of the Treasury is the executive agency responsible for promoting economic prosperity and ensuring US financial security. In addition to advising the President, production of currency, revenue collection and disbursement, the TREAS encourages global economic growth and enhances national security through its economic sanctions against foreign threats to the US and identifying and targeting financial networks that support national security threats. The Secretary of Treasury also represents and serves as the US Governor on the boards of the IMF, World Bank, Asian Development Bank, African Development Bank, European Bank for Reconstruction and Development, and Inter-American Development Bank. The TREAS coordinates policy and information sharing with these and other financial institutions.

Organization Description /Programs	The Office of Terrorism and Financial Intelligence (TFI), with its sub-offices of the Financial Crimes Enforcement Network (FinCEN), Intelligence and Analysis (OIA), and the Foreign Assets Control (OFAC), as well as the Assistant Secretary for Terrorist Financing, uses intelligence and enforcement functions to safeguard the financial system against national security threats. The TREAS, in conjunction with the DEA and the Defense Departments, supports the Afghan Threat Finance Cell (ATFC) which scrutinizes the hawala networks, an informal banking system popular with the Taliban for moving monies quickly and cheaply.
Relevant Regulation	Treasury Order 105-17 established the Office of Terrorism and Financial Intelligence
Guidance/Oversight	Regional offices in the Under Secretary of Treasury for International Affairs coordinate Country Economic Assessments with other Department of Treasury offices (principally the Under Secretary for Terrorism and Financial Intelligence and the Office of Technical Assistance).
Funding	Congress Appropriations
Web address	www.ustreas.gov

US TRADE AND DEVELOPMENT AGENCY	
Organization Description /Programs	An independent foreign assistance agency funded by Congress that supports economic development, American commercial interests in developing and middle-income countries, and US policy objectives concerning development/capacity building by funding technical assistance, feasibility studies, training, orientation visits and business workshops. USTDA uses foreign assistance funds to support investment policy and decision-making in host countries. Funding is for services sourced in the US, though 20% of USTA funding can be used by the US company to subcontract host country organizations. • In 2009, USTDA launched a Regional Infrastructure and Trade Initiative in South Asia that will promote regional transit and trade links between Afghanistan and Pakistan. • Measures the host country development benefits of USTDA activities by whether or not it resulted in implemented infrastructure projects, additional jobs and training for host country personnel, productivity/modern technology improvements to host country, and systematic reforms to improve economic performance of host country.
Relevant Regulation	Foreign Assistance Act, as amended (22 USC 2421)
Guidance/ Oversight	• Director, SECSTATE, US Emb Kabul oversee the USTDA • USTDA oversees international project procurement activities • USTDA performs due diligence on all overseas project sponsors and US contractors and subcontractors • USTDA works with multilateral banks (MDBs) to co-finance technical assistance and feasibility studies

Funding	State Foreign Operations Appropriations
Web address	http://www.ustda.gov http://www.ustda.gov/pubs/brochures/USTDA_USBusinessGuide.pdf

OVERSEAS PRIVATE INVESTMENT CORPORATION	
Organization Description /Programs	An "independent" US agency, OPIC helps US businesses invest overseas and support economic development in new and emerging markets, and US foreign policy. Provides loan guarantees to expand private investment and help manage the risk of direct foreign investment. OPIC has a Board of Directors appointed by the President and US Senate, and an Executive Staff, which can make project decisions independent of the Board. OPIC charges fees for its products and has no net cost to taxpayers. OPIC Programs: • Afghan Growth Finance (AGF) LLC- a US company receiving loans from OPIC. AGF operates a non-bank financial institution in Afghanistan to provide senior loans and equipment leases to small-medium companies whose focus is on agribusiness, light manufacturing, construction and consumer goods and services. • Citibank Microfinance Framework Agreement II – OPIC and Citibank will share credit risk and provide micro-loans to micro-borrowers in the Middle East
	• companies whose focus is on agribusiness, light manufacturing, construction and consumer goods and services. • Citibank Microfinance Framework Agreement II – OPIC and Citibank will share credit risk and provide micro-loans to micro-borrowers in the Middle East
Relevant Regulation	• Foreign Assistance Act of 1961, as amended • Overseas Private Investment Corporation Reauthorization Act of 2009
Guidance/Oversight	• President of OPIC, SECSTATE, US EMB Kabul, SIGAR • Uses the Character Risk Due Diligence Directive (CRDD) and the Terrorist Screening Center (TSC) before providing project support • Extractive Industries Transparency Initiative (EITI) – publication and verification of revenues from oil, gas, and mining, with the goal of funneling revenues to sustainable development and poverty reduction
Funding	State Foreign Operations Appropriations
Web Address	http://www.opic.gov

2. Host Nation Organizations

GOVERNMENT OF THE ISLAMIC REPUBLIC OF AFGHANISTAN	
Organization Description /Programs	President of the Islamic Republic of Afghanistan Hamid KARZAI (since 7 December 2004); Cabinet: 25 ministers. The bicameral National Assembly consists of the Meshrano Jirga or House of Elders (102 seats, one-third elected from provincial councils for four-year terms, one-third elected from local district councils for three-year terms, and one-third nominated by the president for five-year terms) and the Wolesi Jirga or House of People (no more than 249 seats), directly elected for five-year terms. GIRoA does not currently have the capacity to track, manage, or effectively utilize the levels of foreign aid flowing into Afghanistan. Judicial Programs: • National Justice Program- strategy approved by the Ministry of Justice (MoJ) to build Afghan's judicial system. US builds/renovates courthouses, trains judges, and publishes Afghan laws. • Provincial Justice Coordination Mechanism- sub-national justice effort with US assistance to establish the rule of law Executive Programs: • The Independent Directorate for Local Governance (IDLG) - improves sub-national government, strengthening ties between Kabul and provinces/districts. Trains and screens district governors. Also working on a development project priority list for the Provincial Development Plans (PDP)
Relevant Regulation	• The Constitution of the Islamic Republic of Afghanistan (Ratified) January 26, 2004 • Afghanistan National Development Strategy (ANDS)
Guidance/Oversight	• Guidance from the international community • High Office of Oversight- independent oversight unit • Office of the Attorney General has a special investigative unit for anti-corruption
Funding	• 90% of public spending in Afghanistan comes from outside GIRoA, and 70% of GIRoA's total budget comes from international donors. • Reconstruction Trust Fund • Law and Order Trust Fund • DOD-funds Justice sector • USAID- funds Justice sector • International Narcotics Control and Law Enforcement (INCLE) – Justice sector
Web address	https://www.cia.gov/library/publications/the-world-factbook/geos/af.html http://www.state.gov/r/pa/ei/bgn/5380.htm http://www.defense.gov/pubs/OCTOBER_1230_FINAL.pdf

AFGHAN NATIONAL SECURITY FORCES	
Organization Description /Programs	Comprised of the Afghan National Army (ANA) and the Afghan National Police (ANP). NATO ISAF and the DOD support the ANSF through equipment, training, and funding. Goal is to have full Afghan military capability by 2010. Programs: • Focused District Development (FDD) program- improve district Afghan Uniformed Police (AUP) units • Counter narcotics Infantry Kandak (CNIK)- US, in conjunction with Afghan Ministry of Defense (MoD) and Afghan Ministry of Interior (MoI),provides force protection for ANP counter narcotic activities
Relevant Regulation	Afghanistan National Development Strategy (ANDS)
Guidance/Oversight	• US • NATO Training Mission - Afghanistan • Combined Security Transition Command–Afghanistan • ISAF • ANA subordinate to Afghan's Ministry of Defense (MoD)
Funding	• DOD • Afghan Security Forces Fund (ASFF) • Afghan National Army (ANA) Trust Fund (only for ANA use)- covers costs of transporting/installing equipment donations and purchasing equipment, services for engineering and construction projects, and in/out-of-the country training.
Web Address	http://www.gao.gov/htext/d08883t.html http://www.rand.org/pubs/monographs/2009/RAND MG845.pdf http://csis.org/files/publication/100609 ANSF reporting.reform.pdf http://www.defense.gov/pubs/OCTOBER 1230 FINAL.pdf

MINISTRY OF RURAL REHABILITATION AND DEVELOPMENT	
Organization Description /Programs	An independent ministry of GIRoA, with a mission to ensure the social, economic and political well-being of rural society (with emphasis on the poor and vulnerable), through the provision of basic services, by strengthening local governance, and promoting sustainable livelihoods free from a dependency on illicit poppy cultivation. MRRD operates through six national programs. • Afghanistan Rural Enterprise Development Program (AREDP)- national program of MRRD with the initiative of employment/income generation (promote savings and loans) for men and women through supporting rural enterprises. Program was initiated by the World Bank. Implementation principles include, market orientation, sustainable businesses, clients decide, improving coordination, building partnerships, simple design, sharing best practices, and vertical integration. Point of entry into the community thru Community Development Councils (CDCs)

Relevant Regulation	<ul><li>Afghanistan National Development Strategy (ANDS) Benchmark 6.2, 6.3</li><li>Strategic Intent document for MRRD, 2007 Comprehensive Agricultural Rural Development (CARD) initiative</li></ul>
Guidance/Oversight	<ul><li>International Development Association (IDA) of the World Bank</li><li>Multiple bilateral donors (Australia, Canada, Denmark, Finland, Germany, India, Italy, Japan, Sweden, Switzerland, United Kingdom, USA, Spain Asian Development Bank, European Commission (EC), Consultative Group to Assist the Poor (CGAP), International Organization for Migration (IOM), United Nations Development Programme (UNDP), United Nations High Commissioner for Refugees (UNHCR), Special Drawing Rights (SDR), United Nations Children's Fund (UNICEF), World Food Programme (WFP))</li></ul>
Funding	<ul><li>US</li><li>International funding (World Bank, UN, EC, etc.)</li></ul>
Web Address	http://www.mrrd.gov.af/English/index.htm

APPENDIX B
DETAILED DESCRIPTION OF FUNDING RESOURCES

Funding Sources are the sources and conduits or means of translating funds to activities; a system of projects or services intended to meet a need; Focus here is on the programs most utilized in Afghanistan, recognizing that the listing is not all-inclusive.

1. Afghanistan Reconstruction Trust Fund

Jointly managed by the World Bank, Asian Development Bank, Islamic Development Bank, and United Nations Development Program the Afghanistan Reconstruction Trust Fund (ARTF) programmed $640 million in US dollars through GIRoA's budget in 2009. The ARTF has been extended through donor agreement until 2020. Since 2002, ARTF donors have contributed $3 billion in US dollars to investment projects in Afghanistan. http://siteresources.worldbank.org/INTAFGHANISTAN/Resources/Afghanistan-Reconstructional-Trust-Fund/ARTF_Annual_ReportSY1387.pdf

2. Afghanistan Security Forces Fund

a. **Purpose**. Congress provides Afghanistan Security Forces Fund (ASFF) as a means to help Afghanistan transition toward self governance and improved security. Although the purpose of ASFF is similar to that of Title 22 funds used to train and equip foreign forces, ASFF is a special purpose form of Title 10 funds often referred to as "pseudo Title 22" funds. Title 10 funds may not be used for the purpose of supporting the ANSF. Conversely, ASFF cannot be used to support Title 10 requirements for US Soldiers and organizations. The Commanding General of the Combined Security Transition Command - Afghanistan (CSTC-A) has primary US responsibility for training and equipping the ANSF. At the request of CSTC-A, USFOR-A J8 assists in the administration of the ASFF. USFOR-A's ASFF program is made up of the following distinct categories:

(1) Quick Response Fund (QRF) – requirements between $2,000 and $50,000

(2) Quick Response Fund (QRF) – requirements over $50,000

(3) Combat Service Support (CSS) to the Afghanistan Security Forces

(4) Foreseeable or recurring (non-QRF) requirements for ANSF

b. **Process**. ASFF funds are appropriated by the US Congress to the US Army under Title 10. The Secretary of the Army distributes these funds to the Defense Security Cooperation Agency (DSCA). DSCA provides funding to Military Departments Life Cycle Management Commands (LCMCs) for purchases in the continental US (CONUS) (e.g., major end items, weapons, ammunition, and communication needs), as well as to CSTC-A for items that can be procured through the local contracting office, or to fund services performed by the Department of State (DOS) or the United Nations.

(1) CSTC-A's annual program objectives for the force generation and development of the ANSF bridge the gap between the strategic aims of the CSTC-A

Campaign Plan, subordinate development strategies, and budget execution. Baseline requirements are derived from the approved ANSF force structure. Any modifications to these requirements come from the GIRoA, in consultation with CSTC-A. Changes to requirements result either from a change to the security situation as reflected in updated strategic planning documents of the ministries, or from lessons learned through operational experience.

(2) The ASFF is subdivided by Budget Activity Groups for the Afghan National Army, Afghan National Police and Related Activities that include Detainee Operations. Budget activities are then further subdivided into sub-activity groups. Tracking of funds begins at the Budget Activity Group (BAG – e.g., ANA and ANP) and Sub-Budget Activity Group (SAG – e.g., Infrastructure, Equipment/Transportation, Training and Operations, and Sustainment) levels. BAG and SAG funding authorizations for each fiscal year are loaded into the Army's Program Budget Accounting System (PBAS), as well as a database managed locally in Afghanistan. As Memoranda of Request (MORs) are submitted for CSTC-A requirements, funds availability is confirmed by reviewing current funds status. The status of funds and financial decisions are managed using a Program Budget Activity Council (PBAC) process. The CSTC-A PBAC process reviews budget execution rates, un-financed requirement prioritization, and recommendations for command decision on program changes on a monthly basis.

(3) ASFF provides resources towards fulfilling the objectives of Operation ENDURING FREEDOM. Since its inception, the ASFF has enabled the manning, training, and equipping of the Afghan National Security Forces (ANSF), which has provided the security to allow the GIRoA to grow and mature. Since FY 2005, almost $18.67 billion has been made available to the ASFF. This accounts for approximately 47.5% of total US reconstruction assistance in Afghanistan. The majority of funds have been allocated to the ANA and most of those funds have been disbursed for Equipment and Transportation ($4.43 billion), followed by Sustainment efforts ($2.81 billion). Figure B-1 depicts the process utilized in the ASFF program.

3. Coalition Readiness Support Program

a. **Purpose**. DOD is authorized to provide specialized training and to procure supplies and specialized equipment that can be provided or loaned on a non-reimbursable basis to eligible coalition forces supporting US military operations in Iraq and Afghanistan. The SecDef approves the amount of training, supplies, or specialized equipment to be provided to coalition forces supporting United States military operations in Iraq or Afghanistan. This provision, known as the Coalition Readiness Support Program (CRSP), was granted by the Congress for the purposes of:

(1) Facilitating safe and effective deployment of eligible coalition forces supporting of US military operations in Iraq and Afghanistan,

(2) Achieving a cost savings by creating a rotational pool of equipment available for loan on a non-reimbursable basis to eligible coalition forces supporting of US military operations in Iraq and Afghanistan; and,

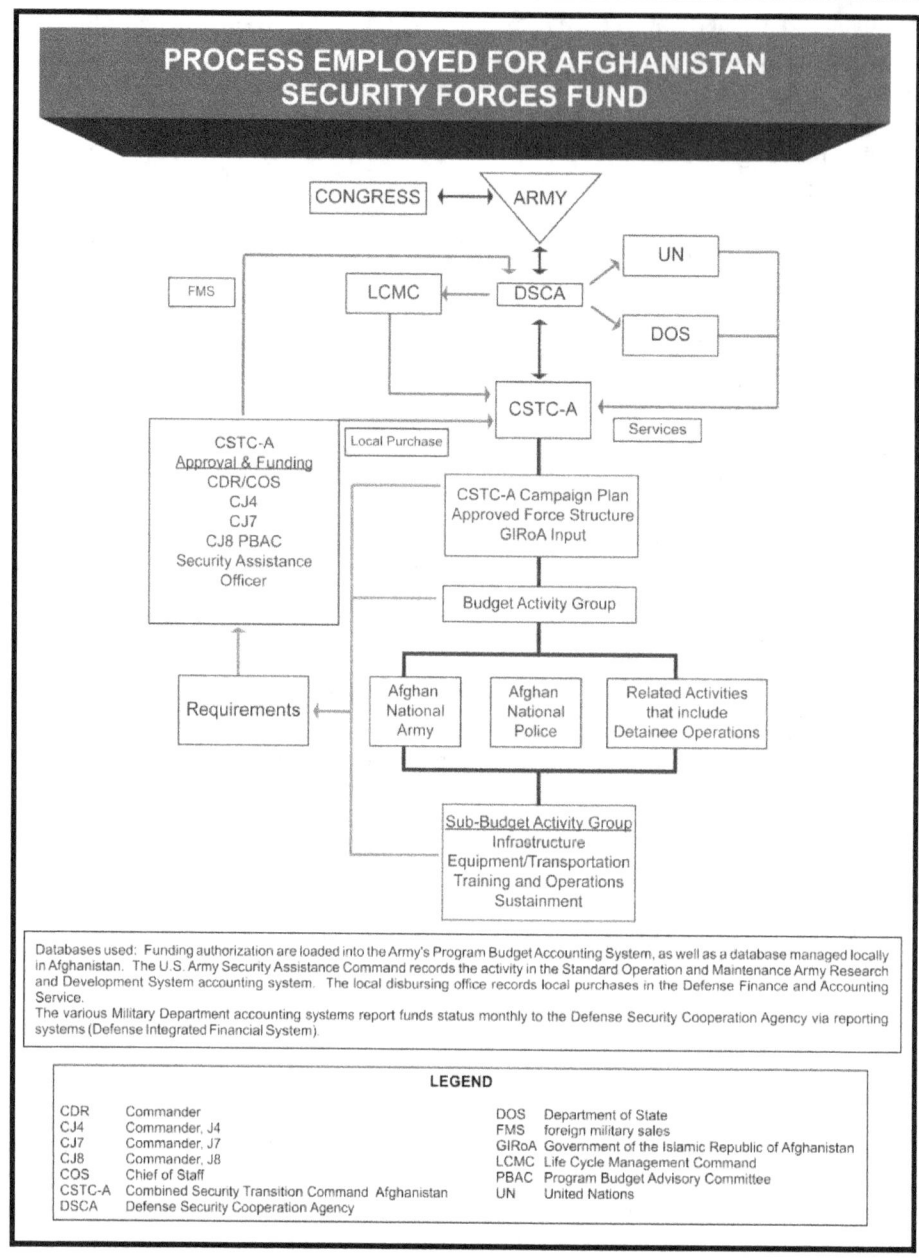

PROCESS EMPLOYED FOR AFGHANISTAN SECURITY FORCES FUND

Databases used: Funding authorization are loaded into the Army's Program Budget Accounting System, as well as a database managed locally in Afghanistan. The U.S. Army Security Assistance Command records the activity in the Standard Operation and Maintenance Army Research and Development System accounting system. The local disbursing office records local purchases in the Defense Finance and Accounting Service.

The various Military Department accounting systems report funds status monthly to the Defense Security Cooperation Agency via reporting systems (Defense Integrated Financial System).

LEGEND

CDR	Commander	DOS	Department of State
CJ4	Commander, J4	FMS	foreign military sales
CJ7	Commander, J7	GIRoA	Government of the Islamic Republic of Afghanistan
CJ8	Commander, J8	LCMC	Life Cycle Management Command
COS	Chief of Staff	PBAC	Program Budget Advisory Committee
CSTC-A	Combined Security Transition Command Afghanistan	UN	United Nations
DSCA	Defense Security Cooperation Agency		

Figure B-1. Process Employed for Afghanistan Security Forces Fund

(3) Ensuring eligible coalition forces supporting of US military operations in Iraq and Afghanistan have current and interoperable safety equipment thus potentially reducing casualties for both coalition and US forces.

b. **Process**. This provision is available to eligible coalition forces who are supporting US operations in Iraq or Afghanistan when the CDRUSCENTCOM or designee verifies the support provided by the coalition forces supports the US military operation. This provision is included within the DOD's appropriation for CSF and as such is subject to financial management procedures established by the Under SecDef (Comptroller). The CRSP is only available at this time to provide specialized training, supplies, and specialized equipment to eligible coalition forces supporting US military operations in Iraq and Afghanistan. These guidelines will be amended if the authority is expanded outside of Iraq and Afghanistan. Before providing specialized training or procuring and providing supplies or specialized equipment to coalition forces, the SecDef will obtain the concurrence of the SECSTATE, consult with the Director of the Office of Management and Budget (OMB), and notify the congressional defense committees 15 days before releasing CSF funding for this purpose. These requirements necessitate careful planning to ensure the processing time, which can take a minimum of eight weeks, is included in operational timelines. DOD is also required to make quarterly reports to the congressional defense committees on the use of CSF funding.

(1) **The Approval Process for Obtaining Funds for Specialized Training**. Specialized training is that essential training required for partner nations to deploy effectively and safely with the US Armed Forces in contingency operations. Examples of specialized training include entry control point training, heavy vehicle driver training, instruction on use of specialized equipment, basic English language training to enable fundamental communication levels, COIN training, and operational training based on an assessment of needs. The procedure for obtaining approval of specialized training involves the following steps conducted in two stages, pre-approval and approval:

(a) **Pre-Approval Stage**

1. The supporting CCDRs should generate a list of standard training requirements for partner nations deploying to contingency operations and work with the Military Departments to coordinate availability and logistics at proposed training sites.

2. The partner nation and the Security Cooperation Office (SCO) (or dedicated office within the US Embassy) begin discussions on the possibility of deploying forces to contingency operations that includes a requirement for specialized training needed to ensure successful deployment of forces.

3. The SCO, working with the supporting CCDR, identifies the training necessary to meet the requirement and starts to develop a proposal based on a country-specific assessment that should include the following:

a. The type of training needed for deployment and the justification for the training;

b. The estimated dates of deployment and numbers of forces who will deploy;

c. The location, duration, and proposed dates of training;

d. Estimated cost of training per person, including itemized charges for course materials, instructors, logistical support, and other costs as appropriate, including transportation to and from the training location;

e. The numbers of forces who require training; and

f. Certification that the forces would not be able to participate in the US military or stability operations but for provision of training.

4. The SCO and supporting CCDR notify the OUSD (Policy), the OUSD (Comptroller), and the supported CCDR of the pending requirement to begin the pre-approval review process, which also includes consultations with the Military Departments, and DSCA.

5. The pre-approval review process results in a specialized training requirement that meets the intent of this guidance and is available from within DOD training resources. The OUSD (Policy) or the OUSD (Comptroller) requests DSCA begin the process of developing a pseudo case for providing the training to the partner nation in the timeframe needed to meet the deployment schedule. DSCA should refer any policy or funding issues to the OUSD (Comptroller) to resolve. OUSD (Comptroller), in coordination with the OUSD (Policy) and OGC (Fiscal), will evaluate and recommend resolution of any issues with regard to the use of CRSP authority.

(b) **Approval Stage**

1. The SCO asks the Ministry of Defense to request the specialized training formally by sending official correspondence to the supported CCDR committing forces to an upcoming deployment to contingency operation. The letter should include the inclusive dates of deployment, the numbers of forces deploying, the mission the forces will conduct in the contingency operation, and the training requirement. The letter should also include a promise to repay the costs of training should the forces not deploy after the training has been provided.

2. Upon receipt of the request for training, the SCO endorses the request as necessary for successful and safe deployment with the US Armed Forces in the contingency operation. The SCO verifies program feasibility with DSCA and confirms pricing with the Military Department security assistance office. The supporting CCDR provides a further endorsement verifying the training is required for deployment. The request and endorsements are sent to the OUSD (Policy), OUSD (Comptroller), DSCA, and the supported CCDR.

3. The supported CCDR validates the partner nation is supporting the US military or stability operation and that training is required for an effective and safe deployment. If the partner nation is deploying as part of ISAF, the supported CCDR (or his/her designee) verifies the support provided by the coalition forces supports the operation. The supported CCDR forwards the documentation to the OUSD (Comptroller) and OUSD (Policy) with a copy to DSCA.

4. The OUSD (Comptroller) and OUSD (Policy) review the request to ensure requirements are consistent with the guidelines and military objectives in the contingency operation and that the request includes sufficient justification to enable development of the SecDef approval that the support by the coalition forces is in connection

with US military operations in the contingency operation and that the provision of training, supplies, or equipment is required for effective deployment. After the evaluation of the documentation, the DSCA will develop the approval package and forward to the OUSD (Comptroller) for coordination and signature by the SecDef.

<u>5</u>. Upon approval by the SecDef and after completion of the 15-day congressional notification period, the OUSD (Comptroller) will release funds to the DSCA to enable implementation of the pseudo case(s).

(2) **The Approval Process for Obtaining Funds for Supplies and Specialized Equipment**. Specialized equipment is procured for the purpose of loaning on a non-reimbursable basis to partner nation forces to ensure an effective and safe deployment in Iraq or Afghanistan. Specialized equipment includes radios, night vision devices, Blue Force Tracker, and Symphony. Maintenance and sustainment of such specialized equipment is also included in this category. Except in extraordinary circumstances, certain items of equipment, including HMMWVs and MRAP vehicles, are not included in this category. Such equipment should be requested under the authority granted to DOD to use the Acquisition and Cross Servicing Agreements to lend military equipment for personnel protection and survivability (Section 1202 of the National Defense Authorization Act for Fiscal Year 2007, as amended). In extraordinary circumstances, military equipment such as vehicles may be requested under the authority through submission of a waiver request to OUSD (Policy) for approval by the DepSecDef. The procedure for obtaining approval of supplies and specialized equipment differs from the training process and involves the following steps accomplished in two stages:

(a) **Pre-Approval Stage**

<u>1</u>. The supported CCDR should develop a standardized set of supplies and interoperable specialized equipment for eligible coalition forces based on missions to be performed. Include in the supplies and specialized equipment set estimated costs for each item, quantity required, and coalition forces to which equipment is expected to be issued. In addition, the supported CCDR should also develop the methods and mechanisms whereby the supplies and equipment will be stored, issued, and inventoried upon return to the pool.

<u>2</u>. The supported CCDR provides the OUSD (Policy), the OUSD (Comptroller), and DSCA the proposed equipment and supply requirements for prioritization, consideration of availability through DOD's procurement processes, and identification of funding. The supported CCDR should validate that the CRSP is the best source to finance the purchase of supplies or equipment.

<u>3</u>. Once the equipment and supply requirements are set, the OUSD (Policy) or the OUSD (Comptroller) requests the DSCA to begin to develop the pseudo cases to enable procurement of the equipment and supplies in time to meet the deployment schedules.

(b) **Approval Stage**

<u>1</u>. The supported CCDR prepares the written validation requesting approval of and funding for the specialized equipment and supplies and forwards the documentation to the OUSD (Comptroller) and the OUSD (Policy).

<u>2</u>. The request is reviewed to ensure requirements are consistent with these guidelines and military objectives in contingency operations and that the request includes sufficient justification to enable approval by the SecDef. The DSCA will develop the approval package and forward to the OUSD (Comptroller) for coordination and signature.

<u>3</u>. Upon approval by the SecDef and after completion of the 15-day congressional notification period, the OUSD (Comptroller) will release funds to the DSCA to enable implementation of the pseudo case.

<u>4</u>. Upon deployment to a contingency operation, the partner nation is issued the required specialized equipment and supplies in accordance with the guidelines established by the supported CCDR for issuing, storing, and accounting for the equipment and supplies.

4. Combatant Commander Initiative Fund

a. In FY 09 Congress provided $50 million for a "CINC Initiative Fund" (now known as the Combatant Commander Initiative Fund [CCIF]) designed specifically to enhance the geographic CCDRs' (GCCs') warfighting capabilities and to be administered by CJCS. CJCS has subsequently directed that these funds only be made available for "Low Cost, High Benefit CINC Requirements" (i.e., joint exercises, force training, contingencies, C2, readiness and sustainability objectives, etc.), and allocated competitively, rather than on a formula basis amongst all of the GCCs. The fund is a means of handling unforeseen requirements that could not be addressed in the normal budget process. CCIF is subject to congressional appropriation and has reflected varying amounts each year. CJCS may withhold a portion of the funds for use in support of GCC contingencies that may arise during the year.

b. **Purpose**. Funds can be authorized by the CJCS for any of the following activities:

(1) Joint exercises (including activities of participating foreign countries) and force training,

(2) Contingencies and selected operations,

(3) Humanitarian and civic assistance, to include urgent and unanticipated humanitarian relief and reconstruction assistance,

(4) C2,

(5) Military education and training to military and related civilian personnel of foreign countries (including transportation, translation, and administrative expenses),

(6) Personnel expenses of defense personnel for bilateral or regional cooperation programs, and

(7) Force protection.

c. **Priority**. The CJCS, in considering requests for funds in the CCDR Initiative Fund, should give priority consideration to:

(1) Requests for funds to be used for activities that would enhance the warfighting capability, readiness, and sustainability of the forces assigned to the commander requesting the funds; and

(2) The provision of funds to be used for activities with respect to an area or areas not within the GCC's area of responsibility (AOR) that would reduce the threat to, or otherwise increase, the national security of the United States.

d. **Relationship to other funding**. Any amount provided by the CJCS during any fiscal year out of the CCDR Initiative Fund for an activity referred to in subsection (b) shall be in addition to amounts otherwise available for that activity for that fiscal year.

e. **Limitations**

(1) Of funds made available under this section for any fiscal year:

(a) Not more than $10,000,000 may be used to purchase items with a unit cost in excess of investment/expense threshold;

(b) Not more than $10,000,000 may be used to pay for any expenses of foreign countries participating in joint exercises as authorized by subsection (b)(5); and

(c) Not more than $5,000,000 may be used to provide military education and training (including transportation, translation, and administrative expenses) to military and related civilian personnel of foreign countries as authorized by subsection (b)(7).

(2) Funds may not be provided under this section for any activity that has been denied authorization by Congress.

f. **Legal Basis**. CJCS 7401.01E is the governing document for submission criteria and amplifying information is provided yearly through the JS J-7 fund manager. Although the fund is managed by CJCS, all funding allocation is approved by OSD. The process takes an average of eight weeks from the time the request is submitted, until the time the funds are transferred from the JS Comptroller to the GCC. From funds made available in any fiscal year for the budget account in the DOD known as the "CCDR Initiative Fund," the CJCS may provide funds to a GCC, upon the request or, with respect to a geographic area or areas not within the GCC's AOR, to an officer designated by the CJCS for such purpose.

5. Combating Terrorism Fellowship Program

a. The Combating Terrorism Fellowship Program (CTFP) was established to meet emerging and urgent defense requirement and directly supports DOD and national goals to build partnerships through targeted, nonlethal combating terrorism (CbT) education and training for mid-level to senior-level foreign military officers, senior NCOs; Ministry Defense officials; and security officials whose responsibilities involve CbT. The program's goal is to build and strengthen a global network of CbT experts and practitioners committed to participation in support of US efforts against terrorists and terrorist organizations. CTFP-funded training should be at the strategic and operational levels.

b. **Purpose**. CTFP funding sends foreign military personnel and civilian security officials to US military educational institutions, seminars and other government programs in order to enhance participant skill sets and abilities to engage in CbT activities. Additionally, CTFP funded programs are conducted in the recipient country in a bilateral or multi-lateral basis by mobile education and training teams; US instructors who go to foreign countries to teach courses to groups of students simultaneously translated into their native language. Finally, CTFP funding is used to fund CbT related programs at the five DOD regional centers as well as approved non-US schools. Created in 2002, the CTFP is considered as a compliment to existing security assistance programs and to fill any shortfalls in the USG's efforts to provide targeted, combating terrorism education assistance. It is funded annually though DOD O&M money managed by DSCA, with oversight from OASD GSA/PS. The goals of CTFP are to:

(1) Augment/enforce USG strategy to build partners' capacity in the Global War on Terrorism (GWOT);

(2) Create a network of CbT experts and practitioners who share common values and a common language in the fight against terrorism; and

(3) To develop the field of countering ideological support for terrorism (CIST).

c. **Legal Basis**. CTFP was authorized in the NDAA for FY05, Public Law 108-136 (10 USC 2249c): §2249c. Authority to use appropriated funds for costs of attendance of foreign visitors under the Regional Defense Counterterrorism Fellowship Program.

(1) **Authority to use Funds**. Under regulations prescribed by the SecDef, funds appropriated to the DOD may be used to pay any costs associated with the attendance of foreign military officers, ministry of defense officials, or security officials at US military educational institutions, regional centers, conferences, seminars, or other training programs conducted under the Regional Defense Counterterrorism Fellowship Program, including costs of transportation and travel and subsistence costs.

(2) **Limitation**. The total amount of funds used under the authority in subsection (a) in any fiscal year may not exceed $20,000,000.

(3) **Annual Report**. Not later than December 1 of each year, the SecDef shall submit to Congress a report on the administration of this section during the fiscal year ended in such year. The report shall include the following matters:

(a) A complete accounting of the expenditure of appropriated funds for purposes authorized under subsection (a), including:

1. The countries of the foreign officers and officials for whom costs were paid; and

2. for each such country, the total amount of the costs paid.

(b) The training courses attended by the foreign officers and officials, including a specification of which, if any, courses were conducted in foreign countries.

(c) An assessment of the effectiveness of the Regional Defense Counterterrorism Fellowship Program in increasing the cooperation of the governments of foreign countries with the United States in the GWOT.

(d) A discussion of any actions being taken to improve the program.

6. Commander's Emergency Response Program

The Commander's Emergency Response Program (CERP) is designed to enable local commanders in Iraq and Afghanistan to respond to urgent humanitarian relief and reconstruction requirements within their operational area by carrying out programs that will immediately assist the indigenous population. As used here, reconstruction does not limit efforts to restore previous conditions/structures in Afghanistan. Also, as used here, urgent is defined as any chronic or acute inadequacy of an essential good or service that, in the judgment of a local commander, calls for immediate action. In addition, the CERP is intended to be used for small-scale projects that, optimally, can be sustained by the local population or government. Small-scale would generally be considered less than $500,000 per project. Projects of $500,000 or more are expected to be relatively few in number and require higher headquarters approval depending on the amount of expenditure. For example, any project over $1 million must be approved by CDRUSCENTCOM. http://comptroller.defense.gov/fmr/12/12_27.pdf. CERP is a major vehicle for funding humanitarian projects, and provides a model for local procurement processes. Figure B-2 provides a depiction of the CERP process.

7. Community Stabilization Program

The Community Stabilization Program (CSP) is a nonlethal COIN program aimed at reducing incentives for participation in violent conflict by employing or engaging at-risk youth, ages 17 to 35, in its many projects. As a three-year program designed to complement broader COIN efforts, CSP is unique and non-traditional for USAID. It nevertheless constitutes its largest cooperative agreement worldwide, with overall funding of $675 million. CSP has four primary components: Short-term employment generation through community infrastructure and essential service projects, long-term job creation through business development programs, education through vocational training and apprenticeships, and engagement through youth activities. http://pdf.usaid.gov/pdf_docs/PDACN461.pdf.

8. Cooperative Threat Reduction Defense and Military Contact Program

a. **Purpose**. The Cooperative Threat Reduction (CTR) Defense and Military Contact (DMC) program aims to develop active and positive relationships between the defense, military, and security communities of the United States and CTR-eligible states of the former Soviet Union (FSU) (Armenia, Azerbaijan, Georgia, Moldova, Russia, Ukraine, Uzbekistan Tajikistan, Kazakhstan, and Kyrgyzstan). CTR legislation (Nunn-Lugar) provides funding for

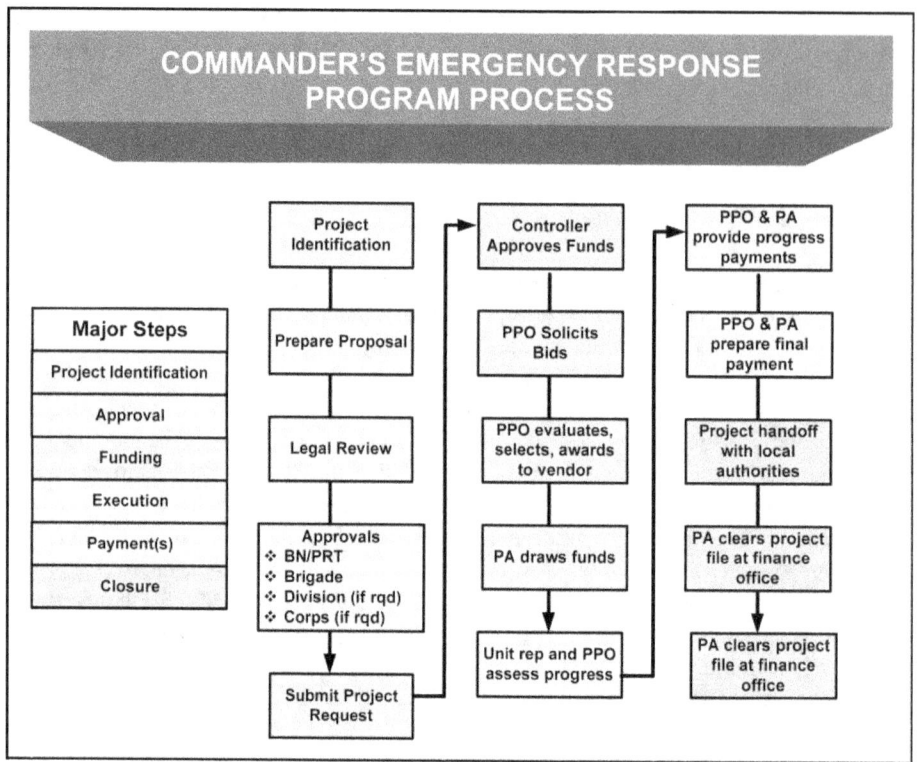

Figure B-2. Commander's Emergency Response Program Process

activities designated as DMC and for military-to-military programs that focus on countering the threat of proliferation of weapons of mass destruction (WMD) with the security forces of CTR-certified states. It contributes to US national security interests by facilitating bilateral and multilateral programs with nations to:

(1) Dismantle FSU WMD and associated infrastructure;

(2) Consolidate and secure FSU WMD and related technology and materials;

(3) Increase transparency and encourage higher standards of conduct;

(4) Support defense and military cooperation with the objective of preventing proliferation;

(5) Stem proliferation of chemical, biological, and nuclear weapons; and

(6) Increase US access to the region by strengthening defense partnerships.

b. **Legal Basis**

(1) **CTR Program Inception**. Soviet Nuclear Threat Reduction Act of 1991 [H.R. 3807] - Section 212 establishes "Authority for program to facilitate Soviet weapons destruction.

(2) **CTR Act of 1993** [NDAA FY94: H.R. 2401, Title XII] expands authorities to multiple program types and establishes program restrictions.

(3) **CTR-DMC Program Inception**. "The Congress finds that it is in the national security interest of the United States for the United States to...[expand] military-to-military and defense contacts between the United States and the independent states of the former Soviet Union." [Sec. 1202/1203]

(4) **CTR-DMC Program Authorities**. NDAA FY96 [S. 1124] specifies limited allocations for "activities designated as Defense and Military Contacts/General Support/ Training in Russia, Ukraine, Belarus, and Kazakhstan."

(5) **NDAA FY97 [H.R. 3220]** "[expands] military-to-military programs of the United States that focus on countering the threat of proliferation of weapons of mass destruction to include the security forces of the independent states of the former Soviet Union, particularly states in the Caucasus region and Central Asia."

(6) **Public Law 110-181 NDAA FY08, Title XII, Sec 1301(c)**. "Availability of Funds - Funds appropriated pursuant to the authorization of appropriations in section 301 for Cooperative Threat Reduction program shall be available for obligation for three fiscal years." Section 907 of the FREEDOM Support Act of 1992 (P.S. 102-511) broadly restricts most assistance to the Government of Azerbaijan, including most military-to-military and intelligence assistance, and hinders the United States from making effective use of Azerbaijan's crucial support in the GWOT. However, Title II of the Foreign Operations, Export Financing, and Related Programs Appropriations Act, 2002 (P.S. 107-115), under the heading "Assistance for the Independent States of the Former Soviet Union," permits the President to waive Section 907 (907 waiver authority) and to extend that waiver on an annual basis if he determines, and certifies to the Committees on Appropriations, that to do so:

(a) Is necessary to support United States efforts to counter terrorism; or

(b) Is necessary to support the operational readiness of United States Armed Forces or coalition partners to counter terrorism; or

(c) Is important to Azerbaijan's border security; and

(d) Will not undermine or hamper ongoing efforts to negotiate a peaceful settlement between Armenia and Azerbaijan, or be used for offensive purposes against Armenia.

(7) On January 25, 2002, the President exercised the 907 waiver authority for the first time, and the waiver has been extended annually since, most recently on March 2008 by the SecDef. The authority to waive this restriction was delegated to the SecDef in Executive Order 13346. The 907 waiver authority requires consultation with the Committees on Appropriation prior to providing any assistance pursuant to a waiver of Section 907. Finally, within 60 days of waiving Section 907, the SecDef must send a report to the appropriate committees detailing the nature and quantity of all training and assistance provided pursuant to the waiver, the status of the military balance between Azerbaijan

and Armenia, the impact of our assistance on that balance, the status of settlement negotiations between Armenia and Azerbaijan and the impact of our assistance on those negotiations.

9. Counter-Narco Terrorism/Counterdrug Support

a. **Purpose**. The USEUCOM Counter Narco-Terrorism (CNT) Division funding is used for partner nation capability enhancement to assist partner nations in training and equipping to combat the threat of drugs and narco-terrorism in their territories. Per the FY05 JSCP direction, CDRUSEUCOM established the CNT Strategic Plan and CONPLAN 4275-05 (CNT Operations) to provide details and guidance to CNT Theater Security Cooperation and operational support. CNT can provide the following types of support:

(1) Maintenance, repair, and upgrade of loaned DOD and other equipment;

(2) Transportation support;

(3) Use of military vessels for law enforcement operation bases;

(4) Establishment and operation of bases of operation of training facilities;

(5) Counterdrug related training of law enforcement personnel;

(6) Detection, monitoring, and communication;

(7) Construction of roads, fences, and installation of lighting at US borders;

(8) Establishment of command, control, and computer networks;

(9) Provision of divers, linguists, intelligence analysis, and tunnel detection support;

(10) Aerial and ground reconnaissance; and

(11) Technology demonstrations.

b **Legal Basis**. Most of the support to CNT is authorized under Title 10 § 1004. Under § 1022, CNT funds may be used to combat terrorism. If a country is approved under § 1033, CNT funds can be used to equip approved partner nations. Criteria for use: Must have a drug nexus for funding.

10. Defense Environmental International Cooperation

a. **Purpose**. The Office of the Deputy Under SecDef (Installations and Environment) (ODUSD(I&E)), in partnership with OSD(Policy) and GCCs, engages in military-to-military cooperation with the ministries of Defense of more than 15 nations to further the security cooperation and US national security goals. Defense Environmental International Cooperation (DEIC) activities and partnering efforts help maintain access to resources, including air, land,

and sea, for training and readiness; minimize encroachment; contribute to interoperability; and foster a global military environmental ethic. The United States partners with foreign militaries to better understand how to evaluate, prioritize, and more effectively meet military environmental, safety and occupational health (ESOH) needs to promote force health protection, reduce US liability and to comply with international environmental treaty obligations overseas. The DOD's environmental activities also assist militaries in newly democratic states with adjusting to concepts such as civilian oversight, public accountability, openness, and cooperation with civilian agencies.

(1) **DEIC Supports DOD's Mission**. DEIC supports US national security and military strategies, as well as foreign and Defense policy goals. Through military-to-military cooperation, DOD seeks to strengthen defense relationships that promote specific US security interests and supports the GWOT; enhance allied and friendly military capabilities for self defense and coalition operations; provide US forces with peacetime and contingency access and en route infrastructure; foster regional stability, democratization, and strong alliances. Defense environmental cooperation activities encourage militaries to discuss regional environmental issues in a neutral forum that helps build trust among militaries. These information exchanges also demonstrate that DOD is a trusted ally, a responsible force, and is committed to protecting the environmental resources entrusted to the DOD by HNs. These efforts help maintain international access to air, land, and sea resources necessary for basing, training, and operations. DOD's environmental international cooperation activities also provide opportunities for USG agencies and industries to better understand the needs and issues impacting foreign militaries and create opportunities for access to foreign environmental research data, technologies, and processes. Examples of cooperation activities include:

(a) Delegation exchanges,

(b) Joint analyses of environmental data,

(c) Information sharing,

(d) Bilateral or multilateral development of ESOH products, such as handbooks, which can be used in promoting ESOH concepts to militaries worldwide, and

(e) Hosting or attending conferences that address military ESOH issues in a regional or multilateral context.

b. **Process**. The following is representative of the annual call for funding from FY07. The Oversight Group of the DEIC program will convene to review and prioritize proposals for FY10 in September 2009 at the Institute for Defense Analyses, Room 6701, 4850 Mark Center Drive, Alexandria, VA. The Oversight Group is comprised of three voting representatives: ODUSD (I&E) ERS, ODASD (Policy/Strategy), and the office of the Director of the Joint Staff. Representatives are welcome to bring additional staff. The meeting will be conducted at the Secret level. Visit requests need to be faxed to Visitor Control, (703) 845-2588 (phone: 703-845-6900) or mailed to Visitor Control at the Institute for Defense Analyses at the above address by September 2, 2010. Results from the Oversight Group will be announced via e-mail. The format of the proposals is as follows:

(1) Title.

(2) Organization originating request, including government action officer, e-mail address, and phone number.

(3) Proposal description, which should include an explanation of how the proposal supports the SECDEF Security Cooperation Guidance, the Combatant Command's Theater Security Cooperation Plan, and relationship to ODUSD (Installations & Environment) priority areas.

(4) Deliverables: as applicable, describe the expected outcome and benefits of the proposals (e.g. handbook, exercise, workshop, proceedings) and exportability of the product (within the region, to other countries, etc.).

(5) Method (e.g. in-house, contract) and schedule for execution (include planning meetings, events and deliverables).

(6) Resource requirements:

(a) Amount of DEIC funding requested and a detailed spreadsheet breakdown showing funds will be spent (e.g., travel, publication costs, contractor support); DEIC is OM&N funding. We do not use it for travel for non-US citizens, official representation funds, equipment purchases, construction, or renovations.

(b) Cost estimate of the entire proposal (not just the DEIC amount), identifying other resource sources that will be required (e.g., TCA, Warsaw Initiative Funds, IMET, CTR, personnel, technology, etc.).

(c) Priority: CCDRs must prioritize their proposal requests if they are submitting more than one.

11. Developing Country Combined Exercise Program

a. **Purpose.** Developing Country Combined Exercise Program (DCCEP) is a way to defray expenses a developing country encounters from participation in a US exercise. The SecDef, after consultation with the SECSTATE, is authorized under Title 10, Section 2010, to pay the incremental expenses that are incurred by a developing country while participating in a multinational exercise. Developing countries are identified from the World Bank list of developing countries. If not considered "High Income," the country is considered eligible for official development assistance. Exercises must enhance US security interests; US exercise objectives must require HN participation; and HN must be unable to pay for required support without US reimbursement of their incremental expenses.

b. **Process.** Funding is approved annually for the following year by OSD based on a two year DCCEP plan submission. EUCOM's DCCEP funding comes from the Army as EUCOM's executive agent. DCCEP will pay for incremental expenses (rations, fuel, training ammunition and transportation) directly resulting from its participation in an approved exercise with the United States. Requests must:

(1) be submitted for the next two fiscal year request/plan by March of the year prior, or an out of cycle request, to the USEUCOM Program Manager;

(2) be coordinated through designated service component executive agent; and

(3) obtain Country Team input for the exercise.

c. **Legal Basis**. United States Code Title 10 - ARMED FORCES Subtitle A - General Military Law, PART III - TRAINING AND EDUCATION CHAPTER 101 - TRAINING GENERALLY Sec. 2010.

12. Development Assistance

Primarily managed by USAID, Development Assistance (DA) programs are designed to advance sustainable, broad-based economic progress and social stability in developing countries, including Afghanistan. DA funds finance long-term projects to provide humanitarian assistance, address environmental issues, improve governance, and promote socio-economic development.

13. DOD HIV/AIDS Prevention Program

a. **Purpose**. In 1999 the United States joined the International Partnership Against HIV/AIDS in Africa (IPAA) to mitigate the HIV pandemic and stop the spread of the AIDS virus. The African continent is the area of the world hardest hit by the HIV/AIDS epidemic, and many militaries are experiencing readiness problems due to high rates of morbidity and mortality among their personnel. The DOD HIV/AIDS Prevention Program (DHAPP) mission is to reduce the incidence of HIV/AIDS among uniformed personnel in selected African nations and beyond. DHAPP assists in developing and implementing military-specific HIV prevention programs and integrate with other USG agencies, NGOs, and UN programs. As executive agent, the DHAPP Management Office at the Naval Health Research Center (NHRC) provides day-to-day direction of the DOD effort. They provide technical assistance for the countries, prepare and deliver periodic reports, and provide the results of assessments to the appropriate Deputy Assistant SecDef (DASD).

b. **Process**. The FY 06 DHAPP Bill language states: Provided, That notwithstanding any other provision of law, of the amount made available under this heading for research, development, test and evaluation, not less than $5,300,000 shall be available for HIV prevention educational activities undertaken in connection with US military training, exercises, and humanitarian assistance activities conducted primarily in African nations. DHAPP allocates funding to countries in each GCC's AOR based on proposals received from a country. The proposals are received from GCCs, Universities, NGOs, and the HN's military and should be vetted through the Country Team (DATT/ODC). These proposals are reviewed by a panel consisting of members from DHAPP, combatant commands, and other experts from the military medical community. Proposals are given a merit score based on their technical merit for accomplishing HIV/AIDS prevention. DHAPP then presents the collective review results from the proposal review committee to the DOD Board of Directors (OSD, OSD Health Affairs, CCDR representatives, PEPFAR) for their decision on the amount of funding a country will receive. A detailed proposal process can be found at: http://www.nhrc.navy.mil/programs/dhapp/proposals.html.

c. **Legal Basis**. P.L. 108-25.

13. Economic Support Fund

The ESF enables USAID programs that advance US interests by helping countries meet short- and long term political, economic, and security needs. Programs range from supporting CT, bolstering national economies, to assisting in the development of effective, accessible, independent legal systems for a more transparent and accountable government.

14. Exercise Related Construction

a. **Purpose**. Exercise Related Construction (ERC) is unspecified minor military construction (MILCON) fund to build or improve semi-permanent facilities with no permanent US presence that supports CJCS-directed exercises conducted OCONUS. The ERC program is specifically designed to support exercise objectives, facilitate resource savings, enhance troop quality of life, and train military engineers. Congress appropriates a separate unspecified minor MILCON line item for ERC. The funding is directed to the Joint Staff which approves all projects and provides funds to the CCDRs for execution. Project planning, design, construction and management are accomplished by the CCDRs and their Service components. Although ERC is driven by US exercise requirements, the program has a distinct engagement value and is a theater security cooperation activity. Facilities built or improved with ERC are often utilized by the HN on a regular basis while US usage is normally limited to exercise timeframes. In addition, troop labor executing an ERC project often has available time to support an HA project in the vicinity of the ERC project site, further contributing to TSC engagement in the HN. Individual ERC projects are limited in cost to $1.5M. Typical costs of $100K to $400K per project promote efficient use of this limited funding throughout the AOR.

For more information on ERC, refer to CJCSI 4600.02, Exercise-Related Construction Program Management.

b. **Legal Basis**. The ERC program is authorized under Title 10, USC Section 2805

15. Foreign Military Financing – Grants

a. **Purpose**. The Foreign Military Financing (FMF) program consists of congressionally appropriated grants and loans which enable eligible foreign governments to purchase US defense articles, services, and training. FMF funds purchases made through the Foreign Military Sales (FMS) program, which manages government-to-government sales. On a much less frequent basis, FMF also funds purchases made through the Direct Commercial Sales (DCS) program, which oversees sales between foreign governments and private US companies. FMF does not provide cash grants to other countries; it generally pays for sales of specific goods or services through FMS or DCS.

b. **Process**. The State Department's Bureau of Political-Military Affairs sets policy for the FMF program, while the DSCA manages it on a day-to-day basis. In USEUCOM Offices of Defense Cooperation (ODC), military personnel and Department of Army General Service (GS) civilian employees in US embassies overseas, play a key role in managing FMF within recipient countries. Some FMF pays for ODC personnel salaries and operational costs.

Congress appropriates funds for FMF through the yearly DOS Foreign Operations Appropriations Act. Once appropriated for a country, FMF remains available until spent in a DSCA and DFAS managed trust fund account; in some cases, unspent FMF grant money can remain "in the pipeline" for years.

c. **Legal Basis**. The FMF program is authorized by sections 23 and 24 of the Arms Export Control Act (P.L. 90-269, or the AECA), as amended. In order to receive assistance through FMF, countries must meet all the eligibility requirements contained in the Foreign Assistance Act and the Arms Export Control Act.

16. Global Peace Operations Initiative

a. **Purpose**. The Global Peace Operations Initiative (GPOI) is designed to meet the world's growing need for well-trained peace operations forces. The US works with lead nations and selected international organizations to support, train, and equip other countries' forces to perform peace operations in accordance with UN standards. The program is a Presidential initiative led by the DOS, in consultation with the DSCA as the executive agent. GPOI is primarily a training program, with infantry or infantry-like battalions as the primary training audience. The goal is to train and equip units for UN peacekeeping missions. The emphasis of GPOI is Africa, where most of the approximately $100M received annually are allocated. Within Europe, however, several recipient countries have been identified: Albania, Bosnia and Herzegovina, Croatia, Georgia, Macedonia, Romania, Southeast Europe Brigade (SEEBRIG), and Ukraine.

b. **Legal Basis**. GPOI funding is provided to DOS through an annual peacekeeping operations appropriation in the Foreign Operations Appropriations Act.

17. Humanitarian Assistance

a. **Purpose**. DOD HA Program(s) are geared toward creating HN access and influence, as well as improving civilian-military cooperation and coordination in humanitarian operations.

b. **Legal Basis**. United States Code TITLE 10 - ARMED FORCES Subtitle A - General Military Law, PART IV - SERVICE, SUPPLY, AND PROCUREMENT CHAPTER 152 - ISSUE OF SUPPLIES, SERVICES, AND FACILITIES Sec. 2551. Humanitarian Assistance. To the extent provided in defense authorization acts, funds authorized to be appropriated to the DOD for a fiscal year for HA shall be used for the purpose of providing transportation of humanitarian relief and for other humanitarian purposes worldwide. To the extent provided in appropriation acts, funds appropriated for humanitarian assistance for the purposes of this section shall remain available until expended.

(1) **Humanitarian Assistance-Other (HAO)**. Section 2561 of Title 10 provides authority for use of Overseas Humanitarian Disaster and Civic Assistance (OHDACA) funds to carry out humanitarian assistance projects—not in conjunction with military exercises. These are DOD funds that are good for two fiscal years.

(2) **Humanitarian Assistance-Excess Property (HAP-EP)**. Section 2561 and 2547 of Title 10 provides authority for DOD to donate excess nonlethal property to

foreign governments and civilian organizations as requested by DOS/DOD personnel in US embassies. These are also OHDACA funds that are good for two fiscal years.

(3) **Humanitarian and Civic Assistance Program (HCA).** Section 401 of Title 10 authorizes USEUCOM components to conduct humanitarian and civic assistance projects while on operational deployments. These are O&M funds that are good for one fiscal year. Each year, the SecDef solicits nominations from the CCDRs for HA projects as outlined above. The approval process usually takes between 6-11 months. Once projects are approved by both DSCA/SOLIC (OSD) and DOS, funding becomes available to execute the projects. The allocation is usually forwarded to the CCDRs in December/January. For OHDACA, funds are approved by ASD-SO/LIC.

(4) **Status Reports.** The SecDef shall submit to the congressional committees specified in subsection (f) an annual report on the provision of HA pursuant to this section for the prior fiscal year. The report shall be submitted each year at the time of the budget submission by the President for the next fiscal year. Each report under this subsection shall set forth the following information regarding activities during the previous fiscal year:

(a) The total amount of funds obligated for humanitarian relief under this section.

(b) The number of scheduled and completed transportation missions for purposes of providing HA under this section.

(c) A description of any transfer of excess DOD nonlethal supplies made available for humanitarian relief purposes under section 2547 of this title. The description shall include the date of the transfer, the entity to whom the transfer is made, and the quantity of items transferred.

(d) **Report Regarding Relief for Unauthorized Countries.** In any case in which the SecDef provides for the transportation of humanitarian relief to a country to which the transportation of humanitarian relief has not been specifically authorized by law, the Secretary shall notify the congressional committees specified in subsection (f) and the Committees on Appropriations of the Senate and House of Representatives of the Secretary's intention to provide such transportation. The notification shall be submitted not less than 15 days before the commencement of such transportation.

c. **Process.** The principle constraint central with all three of the HA programs is that they may only be used to benefit the civilian population. Additionally, each of the programs is limited to a $500K spending cap per project instituted by HA policy-makers. The sum of the other unique constraints of each of the programs are listed below:

(1) **HA-O**

(a) The program funds stand-alone projects focused on disaster mitigation and preparedness.

(b) HA funding is not discretionary and there are several constraints on how it is spent.

(2) HAP-EP

(a) This program provides only excess property directed to DRMOs and transportation/customs costs associated with the distribution of the equipment or materiel.

(b) It does not provide spare parts or the means for procurement of repair parts after issue.

(3) HCA

(a) Projects are carried out by, and must provide training to, the US military.

(b) Beneficiaries must be the HN civilian population.

18. Humanitarian Mine Action

a. **Purpose**. The Overseas Humanitarian, Disaster, and Civic Aid (OHDACA) appropriation funds DOD Humanitarian Mine Action (HMA) activities, formerly referred to as Humanitarian Demining Operations (HDO). HMA has three pillars: Mine Victims Assistance (MVA), Mine Risk Education (MRE), and the Demining capacity building and training in the HMA field.

b. **Legal Basis**. Congressional authority to conduct HMA programs is embedded in the following sections of Title 10 United States Code: 401, 402, 404, 407, 2557 and 2561. HMA is covered under the newly created (FY07) section 407.

c. **Process**. HMA assistance is outlined in USEUCOM Humanitarian Mine Action Instruction 3201.01. Changes in Title 10 have enabled the use of all DOD assets to include civilian personnel to conduct HMA activities.

19. International Military Education and Training

a. **Purpose**. International Military Education and Training (IMET) is a financing mechanism through which the United States pays for the training or education of foreign military and a limited number of civilian personnel. IMET grants are given to foreign governments, which choose the courses their personnel will attend. IMET funding sends students to approximately 150 US military training institutions throughout the United States. A wide variety of courses for US personnel – some 2,000, including topics ranging from War Colleges to helicopter repair to military justice systems – qualify for IMET funding. On occasion, IMET-funded programs are conducted in the recipient country by mobile education and training teams, US instructors who go to foreign countries to teach courses to groups of students simultaneously translated into their native language. Created in 1976, the IMET program is often considered to be the "traditional" US military training program. It is funded though the foreign aid appropriations process and overseen by the DOS, but actually implemented by the DOD. According to Section 541 of the FAA, IMET-funded training is intended:

(1) To encourage effective and mutually beneficial relations and increased understanding between the United States and foreign countries in furtherance of the goals of international peace and security;

(2) To improve the ability of participating foreign countries to utilize their resources, including defense articles and defense services obtained by them from the United States, with maximum effectiveness, thereby contributing to greater self-reliance by such countries; and

(3) To increase the awareness of nationals of foreign countries participating in such activities of basic issues involving internationally recognized human rights.

b. **Legal Basis**. Chapter five of Part II of the Foreign Assistance Act of 1961 (P.L. 87-195), as amended, authorizes the IMET program to provide military education and training to foreign military and civilian personnel.

20. International Narcotics Control and Law Enforcement

International Narcotics Control and Law Enforcement (INCLE) funds are managed by the DOS Bureau of International Narcotics and Law Enforcement Affairs (INL) to advance the rule of law and to combat narcotics production and trafficking. INCLE funds support several INL program groups, including police training, counternarcotics, rule of law, and enhancing the judiciary system.

21. Joint Combined Exchange Training

a. **Purpose**. The funding resource is referred to as 2011 dollars because the Joint Combined Exchange Training (JCET) charter is from 10 USC §2011, DOD Authorization Act FY99 (as amended by FY99 National Defense Authorization Act 1062). The purpose of this enactment, as stated in the 1991 Senate Armed Services Committee Report, is and must be US SOF training, not to render foreign internal assistance or to conduct FID. Accordingly, there must be a clear and articulate link between the training provided and US SOF unit's mission essential tasks. Finally, 10 USC §2011 mandates annual reporting to Congress.

b. **Legal Basis**. 10 USC §2011, Special Operations Forces: Training with Friendly Foreign Forces. Under regulations prescribed pursuant to subsection (c), the commander of the special operations command established pursuant to section 167 of this title and the CCDR may pay, or authorize payment for, any of the following expenses:

(1) Expenses for training SOF assigned to that command in conjunction with training, and training with, armed forces and other security forces of a friendly foreign country.

(2) Expenses for deploying SOF for that training.

(3) In the case of training in conjunction with a friendly developing country, the incremental expenses incurred by that country as the direct result of such training.

c. **Process**. Title 10 USC §2011 authority is separate and distinct from that contained in the Foreign Assistance Act. CDRUSSOCOM is authorized to expend JCET funds to conduct this training. The training must occur overseas. When the foreign nation is a developing nation, CDRUSSOCOM may fund that nation's incremental expenses, if necessary, to conduct §2011 training. CDRUSSOCOM distributes the funds to the four MACOMs (USASOC, AFSOC, MARSOC, and NAVSPECWARCOM). The MACOMs fund the JCETs through their component units.

22. Joint Exercise Transportation Program

a. **Purpose**. The Joint Exercise Transportation Program (JETP) establishes the process for CCDR participation in the Transportation Working Capital Fund (TWCF). The TWCF provides the funding for strategic lift and port handling/inland transportation costs associated with the movement of US forces and equipment to participate in CCDR-approved exercises. The TWCF budget, managed by CDRUSTRANSCOM, is approximately $280 million dollars per year, of which USEUCOM is apportioned about 14%, ($35-$40 million).

23. Military Construction

Congress appropriates Title 10 USC funds for MILCON of permanent improvements separately in annual appropriation acts. MILCON includes "any construction, development, conversion, or extension of any kind carried out with respect to a military installation whether to satisfy temporary or permanent requirements." (10 USC §2801(a)) The definition of a military installation is very broad and includes foreign real estate under the OPCON of the US military. MILCON includes all work necessary to produce a complete and usable facility or a complete and usable improvement to an existing facility. http://www.acq.osd.mil/dpap/pacc/cc/jcchb/chap_3.html#types.

24. Military Personnel Authorization

a. **Purpose**. Military Personnel Authorization (MPA) is used for pay, allowances, individual clothing, subsistence, interest on deposits, gratuities, and permanent change of station travel (including all expenses for organizational movements) for members on active duty. Each Service has unique names and rules for the MPA funds, but generally there are two types: support funded by the RC and support funded by the AC.

b. **RC funding** (IDT/AT) is intended to prepare assigned, part-time Reservists for their wartime missions. This preparation includes training for the assigned position, but also completion of recurring readiness requirements such as medical exams, fitness tests, security clearance updates, and ancillary training requirements. Normally, Reservists are able to provide concurrent support to their AC organization while they complete these requirements. Additionally, there is a small amount of RC funding (AF RPA and Army ADSW) available to assist with requirements directly supporting RC specific missions.

c. **AC funding** also has two general sub-categories: contingency and critical steady state. Generally, contingency funds must be approved through processes that validate their support for OCO missions, while critical steady state funding can be used to support everything but enduring requirements (greater than one year), which would be better suited for a permanent manning billet.

25. Operations and Maintenance Funding

a. **Purpose**. Operations and Maintenance (O&M) appropriations traditionally finance those things whose benefits are derived for a limited period of time, i.e., expenses, rather than investments. O&M appropriations are used to finance "expenses" not related to military personnel or RDT&E. Types of expenses funded by O&M appropriations include: DOD civilian salaries, supplies and materials, maintenance of equipment, certain equipment items, real property maintenance, rental of equipment and facilities, food, clothing, and fuel. When considering O&M appropriations, remember to adhere to the established expense and investment dollar thresholds. The "expense and investment" criteria basically evolve around cost, purpose, and whether the item is considered a "centrally managed/controlled item." Generally, items costing less than $250,000 and not designated for centralized management and asset control are considered "expenses" and are funded with O&M funds.

b. **Legal Basis**. Title 10, USC.

26. Non-proliferation, Anti-terrorism, Demining, and Related Programs

The Non-proliferation, Anti-terrorism, Demining, and Related Program (NADR) appropriation funding is primarily a DOS appropriation administered by Political-Military Affairs Bureau. The Demining activity is administered by the Weapons Reduction and Abatement Office.

27. Overseas Humanitarian, Disaster, and Civic Aid

a. **Purpose**. The Overseas Humanitarian, Disaster, And Civic Aid (OHDACA) appropriation funds DOD HA activities. The use of HA funds is to fund civic relief projects and includes foreign disaster relief and emergency response (e.g., logistics, airlift, search and rescue, humanitarian daily rations, plastic sheeting, tents) and HMA, formerly referred to as HDO.

b. **Legal Basis**. Congressional authority to conduct programs are embedded in the following sections of Title 10 USC: 401, 402, 404, 407, 2557 and 2561. HMA is covered under the newly created (FY07) section 407.

28. President's Emergency Plan for AIDS Relief

a. **Purpose**. . Under the direction of the US DOS, Office of the Global AIDS Coordinator (OGAC), the President's Emergency Plan for AIDS Relief (PEPFAR) is implemented by multiple

USG agencies working with international, national, and local leaders worldwide to support integrated prevention, treatment and care programs (http://www.pepfar.gov). PEPFAR provides $48 billion to assist foreign countries in combating HIV/AIDS, tuberculosis, and malaria. The primary implementing USG agencies include:

(1) DOS,

(2) USAID,

(3) DOD (US Navy through the Naval Health Research Center is the Executive Agent for management of DOD HIV/AIDS Prevention Program activities in foreign militaries),

(4) Department of Commerce,

(5) Department of Labor,

(6) DHHS, and

(7) Peace Corps.

b. **Legal Basis**. Public Law No: 110-293 The Tom Lantos and Henry J. Hyde United States Global Leadership Against HIV/AIDS, Tuberculosis, and Malaria Reauthorization Act of 2008 and Title 22 USC Chapter 83 - United States Leadership Against HIV/AIDS, Tuberculosis, and Malaria

c. **Process**. Funding requests are submitted via the Country Team/ODC/DATT through a proposal called a Common Operating Plan (COP) or Mini COP to support their partner nation's military HIV/AIDS project. These proposals are worked at the US Embassy Country Team level. The COPs are submitted in the last quarter of a fiscal year and typically reviewed in the first quarter of the new fiscal year. The Mini COPs are submitted at the end of the first quarter of a fiscal year and reviewed in the second quarter of the fiscal year. The COP and mini COP proposals are review by a committee consisting of representatives from DOS, DOD, USAID, CDC, etc and recommendations forward on for further review and approval. Once approved the funding for the DOD project flows from DOS to OSD Health Affairs via a MOU, then to Bureau of Medicine and Surgery (BUMED) and the Naval Health Research Center/ DHAPP.

29. Global Train and Equip

a. **Purpose**. NDAA FY10 Section 1206 gives authority to the SecDef, with concurrence by the SECSTATE, to conduct or support a program or programs to build the capacity of a foreign country's national military forces. Training and equipping foreign national military forces is provided in order for that country to: a) conduct CT operations, or b) participate in or support military and stability operations in which US Armed Forces are a participant (to include operations in Iraq or Afghanistan).

b. **Legal Basis**. Section 1206 funding is authorized via renewing legislation in the annual NDAA. Therefore, the program should not be considered as a consistent funding stream, as it could be terminated unexpectedly.

c. **Process**. Proposals remedying ODC/component-identified capability gaps are submitted to the CCDR for strategy review and prioritization. Selected proposals are sent to SecDef for final approval and to SECSTATE for concurrence. OSD will forward approved projects to Congress for final approval and funding authorization. **No planning/projects can begin nor promises be made to partner nations until Congress authorizes the funding.**

30. Traditional Combatant Commander Activities

a. **Purpose**. Traditional CCDR Activities (TCA) are intended to promote regional security and other US national security goals. TCA are one of the pillars of our Foreign Military Interaction (FMI) initiatives, and TCA fulfill the CCDR's need for flexible resources to interact with the militaries in their AOR in order to promote regional security and other national security goals. TCA are not intended to replace or duplicate any other specifically authorized or appropriated fund sources available to the CCDRs.

b. **Legal Basis**. Title 10 Section 168.

c. **Process**

(1) TCA can be used to fund any O&M and MILPERS activity for which the CCDR currently has authority. Examples include:

(a) Military liaison teams,

(b) Traveling contact teams,

(c) State partnership programs,

(d) Regional conferences and seminars,

(e) Personnel and information exchanges,

(f) Unit exchanges,

(g) Staff assistance/assessment visits,

(h) Training program review and assessments,

(i) Ship rider programs,

(j) Joint/combined exercise observers, and

(k) Combined exercises, though not primarily intended for such exercises.

(2) Though not primarily intended for such use, Humanitarian Civic Assistance (HCA) projects, IAW 10 USC 401 and DOD Directive 2205.2, may be funded, but only for incidental costs of carrying out such assistance as identified in paragraph (C)(2) of 10 USC 401. Examples include:

(a) Bilateral staff talks.

(b) HN medical and dental support planning meetings, not actual medical and dental support.

(c) Program administration, to include supplies and equipment, travel, and translation services.

APPENDIX C
REFERENCES

1. United States Government Laws and Reports

a. U.S. Congress. *Duncan Hunter National Defense Authorization Act for Fiscal Year 2009.* Public Law 110-417, 110th Cong., 2d sess., October 14, 2008. http://www.dod.gov/dodgc/olc/docs/2009NDAA_PL110-417.pdf.

b. U.S. Congress. *National Defense Authorization Act for Fiscal Year 2010.* Public Law 111-84. 111th Cong., 1st sess., October 28, 2009. http://frwebgate.access.gpo.gov/cgi-bin/getdoc.cgi?dbname=111_cong_public_laws&docid=f:publ084.111.pdf.

c. U.S. Congress. *National Defense Authorization Act for Fiscal Year 2008.* Public Law 110-181. 110th Cong., 2d sess., January 28, 2008. http://frwebgate.access.gpo.gov/cgi-bin/getdoc.cgi?dbname=110_cong_public_laws&docid=f:publ181.110.pdf.

d. U.S. Congress. House. Subcommittee on National Security and Foreign Affairs of the Committee on Oversight and Government Reform. *Warlord, Inc.: Extortions and Corruption Along the U.S. Supply Chain in Afghanistan.* 111th Cong., 2nd sess., 2010. http://www.oversight.house.gov/images/stories/subcommittees/NS_Subcommittee/6.22.10_HNT_HEARING/Warlord_Inc_compress.pdf

e. U.S. Government Accountability Office (GAO). *International Security: DOD and State Need to Improve Sustainment Planning and Monitoring and Evaluation for Section 1206 and 1207 Assistance Programs.* GAO-10431, Washington DC: Government Printing Office, April 15, 2010. http://www.gao.gov/new.items/d10431.pdf.

f. U.S. Government Accountability Office (GAO). *Iraq and Afghanistan: Agencies Face Challenges in Tracking Contracts, Grants, Cooperative Agreements, and Associated Personnel.* GAO-10-509T, Washington DC: Government Printing Office, March 23, 2010. http://www.gao.gov/new.items/d10509t.pdf.

g. U.S. Government Accountability Office (GAO). *Military Operations: Actions Needed to Improve Oversight and Interagency Coordination for the Commander's Emergency Response Program in Afghanistan.* GAO-09-615, Washington DC: Government Printing Office, May 2009. http://www.gao.gov/new.items/d09615.pdf.

h. Commission on Wartime Contracting. "Commission on Wartime Contracting In Iraq and Afghanistan." http://www.wartimecontracting.gov/.

i. United States Institute of Peace. *Guidelines for Relations between U.S. Armed Forces and Non Governmental Humanitarian Organizations in Hostile or Potentially Hostile Environments.* Washington DC: United States Institute of Peace. http://www.usip.org/files/resources/guidelines_pamphlet.pdf.

j. Special Inspector General for Afghanistan Reconstruction. *Quarterly Report to the United States Congress.* Arlington, VA: SIGAR, October 30, 2009.

2. Department of Defense Issuances

a. DOD 1322.18. *Military Training.* Department of Defense, January 13, 2009. http://www.dtic.mil/whs/directives/corres/pdf/132218p.pdf.

b. DOD 5105.38-M. *Security Assistance Management Manual. www.dsca.mil/samm/.*

c. DODI 2205.02. *Humanitarian and Civic Assistance (HCA) Activities.*

d. *The Military Support to Stabilization, Security, Transition, and Reconstruction Operations Joint Operating Concept, Version 2.0.* Department of Defense, December 2006. www.dtic.mil/future**joint**warfare/**concepts/sstro_joc**_v20.doc.

e. *Contingency Contracting: A Joint Handbook for the 21st Century.* Department of Defense, Defense Procurement and Acquisition Policy. http://www.acq.osd.mil/dpap/pacc/cc/jcchb/.

3. Chairman of the Joint Chiefs of Staff Issuances

a. CJCSI 2120.01A, *Acquisition and Cross Servicing Agreements.*

b. *Capstone Concept for Joint Operations, Version 3.0.* CCJO v3.0, Department of Defense, January 15, 2009. http://www.jfcom.mil/newslink/storyarchive/2009/CCJO_2009.pdf.

c. *Irregular Warfare (IW) Joint Operating Concept (JOC), Version 1.0.* Department of Defense, September 11, 2007. http://www.dtic.mil/futurejointwarfare/concepts/iw_joc1_0.pdf.

4. Non-Department of Defense Agency Issuances

a. Office of the Coordinator for Reconstruction & Stabilization. "Mission Statement." Department of State Coordinator for Reconstruction & Stabilization website, May 20, 2010. http://www.crs.state.gov/index.cfm?fuseaction=public.display&shortcut=4QXJ.

b. Office of the Coordinator for Reconstruction & Stabilization. "Structure." Department of State Coordinator for Reconstruction & Stabilization website, May 20, 2010. http://www.crs.state.gov/index.cfm?fuseaction=public.display&shortcut=CKIH.

c. Military Affairs. "Tactical Conflict Assessment Framework." USAID. http://www.usaid.gov/our_work/global_partnerships/ma/tcaf.html.

d. Military Affairs. "Training for Provincial Reconstruction Teams." USAID. http://www.usaid.gov/our_work/global_partnerships/ma/prt.html.

e. United States Agency for International Development. *ADS Chapter 102: Agency Organization*. USAID, February 24, 2006. http://www.usaid.gov/policy/ads/100/102.pdf.

f. United States Agency for International Development. *ADS Chapter 103: Delegations of Authority*. USAID, February 18, 2010. http://www.usaid.gov/policy/ads/100/103.pdf.

g. *Standard Operating Procedures (SOP) for Field Ordering Officers*. Contract Operations – Afghanistan, October 2008.

5. Joint Publications, Directives, and Papers

a. JP 4-10. *Operational Contract Support*. Joint Chiefs of Staff, October 17, 2008. http://www.dtic.mil/doctrine/new_pubs/jp4_10.pdf.

b. United States Joint Forces Command. *Handbook for Military Support to Economic Stabilization*. Unified Action Handbook Series, Book Four, February 27, 2010.

c. United States European Command. *Handbook of Theater Security Cooperation Resources*, February 2010.

d. Eikenberry, Karl W., and Stanley A. McChrystal. *United States Government Integrated Civilian Military Campaign Plan for Support to Afghanistan*. USFOR-A & US Embassy Kabul, August 10, 2009.

e. MacDonald, John A. General John A. MacDonald Memorandum for Chief of Staff USJFCOM, "Institutionalizing the Concept of Money as a Weapon System (MAAWS)," 9 May 2009.

f. Petraeus, David. General David Petraeus Memorandum to Multi-National Force Iraq, 21, June 2008.

6. Army Publications and Lessons Learned

a. *FM 3 07. Stability Operations*. Headquarters, Department of the Army. October 2008. http://usacac.army.mil/cac2/repository/FM307/FM3-07.pdf.

b. Center for Army Lessons Learned. *Assessment and Measures of Effectiveness in Stability Ops Handbook: Tactics, Techniques, and Procedures*. No. 10-41, Leavenworth, KS: Center for Army Lessons Learned, May 2010. http://usacac.army.mil/cac2/call/docs/10-41/10-41.pdf.

c. Center for Army Lessons Learned. *Commanders Emergency Response Program: Tactics, Techniques, and Procedures*. No. 08-12, Ft. Leavenworth, KS: Center for Army Lessons Learned, March 2008.

d. Center for Army Lessons Learned. *Commanders Guide to Money as a Weapons System: Tactics, Techniques, and Procedures.* No. 09-27, Ft. Leavenworth, KS: Center for Army Lessons Learned, 2009. http://usacac.army.mil/cac2/call/docs/09-27/toc.asp.

e. Center for Army Lessons Learned. *Deployed COR: Contracting Officer's Representative Handbook: Tactics, Techniques, and Procedures.* No. 08-47, Ft. Leavenworth, KS: Center for Army Lessons Learned, September 2008.

f. Center for Army Lessons Learned. *Field Ordering Officer and Paying Agent Handbook: Tactics, Techniques, and Procedures.* No. 09-16, Leavenworth, KS: Center for Army Lessons Learned, July 2009. http://usacac.army.mil/CAC2/CALL/docs/09-16/09-16.pdf.

g. Center for Army Lessons Learned. *PRT Playbook Handbook: Tactics, Techniques, and Procedures.* No. 07-34, Leavenworth, KS: Center for Army Lessons Learned, September 2007. http://usacac.army.mil/cac2/call/docs/07-34/07-34.pdf.

h. Center for Army Lessons Learned. *Unit Commander's Guide to Paying Agents Handbook.* No. 10-39, Leavenworth, KS: Center for Army Lessons Learned, April 2010. http://usacac.army.mil/cac2/call/docs//10-39/10-39.pdf.

7. United Nations Issuances

a. United Nations. "Charter of the United Nations: Chapter 1; Purposes and Principles." United Nations. http://www.un.org/en/documents/charter/chapter1.shtml.

b. United Nations. "Mandate." United Nations. http://unama.unmissions.org/Default.aspx?tabid=1742.

c. United Nations." Structure and Organization." United Nations. http://www.un.org/en/aboutun/structure/index.shtml.

8. Academic Resources

a. AKSS- Ask a Professor. "Welcome to Ask a Professor!" Defense Acquisition University https://akss.dau.mil/askaprof-akss/.

b. Defense Acquisition University. "DAU Home page." Defense Acquisition University. http://www.dau.mil/.

c. Defense Institute of Security Assistance Management, *The Management of Security Assistance.* The Twenty-Ninth Edition, Wright-Patterson AFB, Ohio. January 2010. www.disam.dsca.mil/DR/29th%20Gbook.pdf.

d. Malkasian, Carter and Gerald Meyerle. *Provincial Reconstruction Teams: How Do We Know They Work.* Carlisle, PA: Strategic Studies Institute, March 2009. http://www.strategicstudiesinstitute.army.mil/pdffiles/PUB911.pdf.

9. Books and Articles

a. Hunt, James P. The 800-Pound Gorilla and Stability Operations. *Small Wars Journal* (June 30, 2010). http://smallwarsjournal.com/blog/2010/06/print/the-800pound-gorilla-and-stabi/.

b. Islamic Republic of Afghanistan. *Afghanistan National Development Strategy: 1387 – 1391 (2008 – 2013); A Strategy for Security, Governance, Economic Growth and Poverty Reduction.* Kabul, Afghanistan: Gul Khana Palace, 2008.

c. Lee, Mark W. "The Commander's Emergency Response Program: Synergistic Results Through Training. *Army Sustainment* 42, no. 3 (May-June 2010). http://www.almc.army.mil/alog/synergy_thrutrain.html.

d. Long, William. "Joint Contingency Contracting: A Step Forward." *Defense AT&L*, May-June 2010. http://www.dau.mil/pubscats/ATL%20Docs/May-Jun10/long_may-june10.pdf.

e. Luck, Gary, and Mike Findlay. *Interagency, Intergovernmental, Nongovernmental, and Private Sector Coordination, Focus Paper #3, 2nd ed.* Joint Warfighting Center United States Joint Forces Command, February 2009. https://jko.cmil.org/file/124/view.

f. NATO-News. "Provincial Reconstruction Teams Look at Way Forward in Afghanistan." NATO, March 16-17, 2010. http://www.nato.int/cps/en/SID-2296AC14-289F6401/natolive/news_62256.htm.

g. Non-Governmental Organization/DPI. "About NGO Association with the UN." United Nations DPI-NGO. http://www.un.org/dpi/ngosection/about-ngo-assoc.asp.

h. Wojciechowski, Mark. "CIDNE Empowers Theater-wide Communication." *USASOC News Service*, February 14, 2006. http://news.soc.mil/releases/News%20Archive/2006/06FEB/060214-02.html.

10. Online Resources

a. ISS Intelligent Software Systems. "CIDNE." ISS. http://www.issinc.com/solutions/cidne.html.

b. Joint Knowledge Online (JKO). JKO Homepage. http://jko.jfcom.mil/, http://jko.jwfc.jfcom.smil.mil , http://jko.cmil.org.

Intentionally Blank

APPENDIX D
ENDNOTES

[1]*Capstone Concept for Joint Operations (CCJO) v3.0*, 15 January 2009, p.21. http://www.dtic.mil/futurejointwarfare/concepts/approved_ccjov3.pdf

[2]General David Petraeus, Memorandum to Multi-National Force Iraq, 21 June 2008. http://usacac.army.mil/CAC2/MilitaryReview/Archives/English/MilitaryReview_20081031_art004.pdf

[3]This guide uses the term "concept" in its generic sense, as an idea, not as a fully vetted operational or integrating concept in the context of the Joint Concept Integrations Development System (JCIDS).

[4]CTF activities include, but are not limited to, countering narcotics trafficking, proliferation activities, (weapons of mass destruction) WMD networks, trafficking in persons, weapons trafficking, precursor chemical smuggling, terrorist revenue and logistics, and other such activities that generate revenue through illicit networks.

[5]SIGAR, *Report of the Special Inspector General for Afghanistan Reconstruction* (October 30, 2009), p. 7. http://www.sigar.mil/pdf/quarterlyreports/Oct09/pdf/SIGAROct2009Web.pdf

[6]The model is intended to have global application; therefore, the elements are broadly based. The segmentation into the six steps of the model used here provides but one possible representation. The number of steps adopted should not be considered inflexible; conditions will dictate if some should be combined or others added.

[7]There is no *doctrine* among civilian departments and agencies for IFO. Two sources of *guidance* for USAID programs are its *Guide to Economic Growth in Post Conflict Countries (January 2009)* http://pdf.usaid.gov/pdf_docs/PNADO408.pdf and *Building Fiscal Infrastructure in Post Conflict Societies* (November 2007) http://pdf.usaid.gov/pdf_docs/PNADK908.pdf.

[8]Joint Publication 1-02, *Department of Defense Dictionary of Military and Associated Terms* (April 21, 2001), p. 74. http://www.dtic.mil/doctrine/new_pubs/jp1_02.pdf

[9]Ibid, p. 343.

[10]CALL, *Commander's Guide to Money as a Weapons System*, (April 2009). http://usacac.army.mil/cac2/call/docs/09-27/09-27.pdf

[11]This is a growing concern in Congress. See for example the recent report issued by the minority staff of the Subcommittee on National Security and Foreign Affairs of the US House of Representatives, *Warlord, Inc.: Extortion and Corruption Along the US Supply Chain in Afghanistan* (June 2010). http://www.oversight.house.gov/images/stories/subcommittees/NS_Subcommittee/6.22.10_HNT_HEARING/Warlord_Inc_compress.pdf

[12]Congress, concerned with systemic problems in defense contracting for Iraq and Afghanistan, established the *Commission on Wartime Contracting in Iraq and Afghanistan*, and has

released several interim reports that identify some of the Commission's initial finding and recommendations. See here: http://www.wartimecontracting.gov

[13]Existing guidance will be found in the *Mission Performance Plan (MPP)* that is prepared for and approved by the US ambassador in-country. The MPP is a loose equivalent to a commander's guidance in that the Ambassador is the Chief-of-Mission for all USG personnel in a country and serves as the personal representative of the president to that country.

[14]Major James P. Hunt, "The 800-Pound Gorilla and Stability Operations," *Small Wars Journal* (June 30, 2010). http://smallwarsjournal.com/blog/journal/docs-temp/464-hunt.pdf

[15]Others include the US Treasury Department, Overseas Private Investment Corporation, US Trade and Development Agency, US Department of Agriculture, the Millennium Challenge Corporation, and the US Commerce Department.

[16]US Department of State, "Department Mission Statement," http://www.state.gov/documents/organization/132214.pdf

[17]The US does not have official diplomatic relations with some countries, e.g., Iran and North Korea., and therefore no embassy accredited to the foreign government. In these cases, the US negotiates through third parties such as Switzerland or Canada.

[18]The list is rather extensive and includes all six regional bureaus that increasingly direct funding of overseas programs; the Bureau for International Narcotics and Law Enforcement; the Under Secretary for Economic, Energy and Agricultural Affairs; the Bureau for Political-Military Affairs that closely coordinates with DOD on, among other issues, foreign military sales and financing; the Under Secretary for Democracy and Global Affairs; and, various independent offices that coordinate budgets and programs such as the Office of US Foreign Assistance, the Office of the Coordinator for Counterterrorism and the Offices of the Global AIDS Coordinator, Global Women's Issues, International Energy, and War Crimes. *All* are stakeholders of varying influence on IFO matters.

[19]Office of the Coordinator for Reconstruction & Stabilization, "Mission Statement," http://www.state.gov/s/crs/about/index.htm.

[20]Ibid.

[21]The roles, responsibilities, authorities and resources of Special Coordinators or "Czars", who generally oversee policy coordination in a region and not merely one country, is still very unclear both within the Executive and Legislative Branches.

[22]United Nations, "Charter of the United Nations: Chapter 1; Purposes and Principles," http://www.un.org/en/documents/charter/chapter1.shtml

[23]United Nations, "Mandate," http://www.un.org/apps/news/story.asp?NewsID=34151&Cr=afghan&Cr1.

[24]Non-Governmental Organization/DPI, "About NGO Association with the UN," http://www.un.org/dpi/ngosection/about-ngo-assoc.asp.

[25]NATO-News, "Provincial Reconstruction Teams Look at Way Forward in Afghanistan," NATO website, (March 16-17, 2010). http://www.nato.int/cps/en/SID-3115AEA1-24FBA99A/natolive/news_62256.htm?

[26]Carter Malkasian and Gerald Meyerle, *Provincial Reconstruction Teams: How Do We Know They Work* (March 2009). http://www.strategicstudiesinstitute.army.mil/pubs/download.cfm?q=911

[27]Ibid.

[28]Major James P. Hunt, The 800-Pound Gorilla and Stability Operations, *Small Wars Journal* (June 30, 2010). http://smallwarsjournal.com/blog/journal/docs-temp/464-hunt.pdf

[29]CALL, *PRT Playbook Handbook*, No. 07-34 (September 2007). http://usacac.army.mil/cac2/call/docs/07-34/07-34.pdf

[30]United States Institute for Peace, *Guidelines for Relations between US Armed Forces and Non Governmental Humanitarian Organizations in Hostile or Potentially Hostile Environments.* http://www.usip.org/files/resources/guidelines_pamphlet.pdf

[31]SIGAR, *Quarterly Report to the United States Congress* (October 30, 2009). http://www.sigar.mil/pdf/quarterlyreports/Oct09/pdf/SIGAROct2009Web.pdf

[32]National Defense Authorization Act (NDAA) for Fiscal Year 2008, (2007), sec. 861, b4. http://frwebgate.access.gpo.gov/cgi-bin/getdoc.cgi?dbname=110_cong_bills&docid=f:h4986enr.txt.pdf

[33]National Defense Authorization Act (NDAA) for Fiscal Year 2009, (2008), sec. 854,. http://frwebgate.access.gpo.gov/cgi-bin/getdoc.cgi?dbname=110_cong_bills&docid=f:s3001enr.txt.pdf

[34]National Defense Authorization Act (NDAA) for Fiscal Year 2010, (2009), sec. 813, a. http://frwebgate.access.gpo.gov/cgi-bin/getdoc.cgi?dbname=111_cong_bills&docid=f:h2647enr.txt.pdf

[35]ISS, "CIDNE", http://www.issinc.com/solutions/cidne.html.

[36]Wojciechowski, Mark, "CIDNE Empowers Theater-wide Communication", USASOC News Service (February 14, 2006). http://news.soc.mil/releases/News%20Archive/2006/06FEB/060214-02.html

[37]GAO, *Iraq and Afghanistan; Agencies Face Challenges in Tracking Contracts, Grants, Cooperative Agreements, and Associated Personnel*, GAO-10-509T (March 23, 2010). http://www.gao.gov/new.items/d10509t.pdf

[38]Karl W. Eikenberry and Stanley A. McChrystal, *United States Government Integrated Civilian Military Campaign Plan for Support to Afghanistan* (August 10, 2009). http://www.comw.org/qdr/fulltext/0908eikenberryandmcchrystal.pdf

[39]Ibid.

[40]Islamic Republic of Afghanistan, *Afghanistan National Development Strategy* (2008-2013). http://www.embassyofafghanistan.org/documents/Afghanistan_National_Development_Strategy_eng.pdf

[41]Islamic Republic of Afghanistan, *Afghanistan: The London Conference* (January 28, 2010). http://afghanistan.hmg.gov.uk/en/conference/london-conference

[42]SIGAR, *Quarterly report to Congress* (October 30, 2009). http://www.sigar.mil/pdf/quarterlyreports/Oct09/pdf/SIGAROct2009Web.pdf

[43]Ibid.

[44]*Civil Military Operations*, JP 3-57, xviii. Members of a CMOC may include representatives of US military forces, OGAs, IPI, IGOs, the private sector, and NGOs. One construct is for the CMOC to report to the JTF chief of staff, rather than to a specific headquarters J-code. http://www.dtic.mil/doctrine/jel/new_pubs/jp3_57.pdf

[45]Ibid.

[46]Under Secretary of State Thomas R. Pickering, Exercise EMERALD EXPRESS 1998. Cited in JP3-57, II-27

[47]For more information on research regarding the assessment of aid as it relates to COIN, see https://wikis.uit.tufts.edu/confluence/display/FIC/Feinstein+International+Center and http://igcc.ucsd.edu/.

[48]CALL, *Assessment and Measures of Effectiveness in Stability Ops Handbook* (May 2010), p. i. http://usacac.army.mil/cac2/call/docs/10-41/10-41.pdf

[49]GAO, *Military Operations; Actions Needed to Improve Oversight and Interagency Coordination for the Commander's Emergency Response Program in Afghanistan*, GAO Report 09-615 (May 2009). http://www.gao.gov/new.items/d09615.pdf

[50]Joint Publication 4-10, *Operational Contract Support* (October 17, 2008), p. iii-2. http://www.dtic.mil/doctrine/new_pubs/jp4_10.pdf

[51]CALL, *Deployed COR: Contracting Officer's Representative Handbook* (September 2008). http://www.acq.osd.mil/dpap/ccap/cc/docs/DCCORH_full_6-30-10.pdf

[52]CALL, *Field Ordering Officer and Paying Agent Handbook* (July 2009). http://usacac.army.mil/cac2/call/docs/09-16/09-16.pdf

[53]CALL, *Commander's Emergency Response Program Handbook* (March 2008). http://info.publicintelligence.net/CERP-Handbook.pdf

[54]John Warner National Defense Authorization Act FY 2007, Public Law No 109-364, sec. 854, (October 17, 2006) mandated four areas that needed to be addressed in terms of joint policy: requirements definition, contingency program management, and contingency contracting. http://frwebgate.access.gpo.gov/cgi-bin/getdoc.cgi?dbname=109_cong_bills&docid=f:h5122enr.txt.pdf

[55]National Defense Authorization Act FY 2008, Public Law No 110-181, sec. 849, (January 28, 2008), added the additional requirement of training all military personnel outside the acquisition workforce, but will have acquisition duties including oversight of contracts or contractors during combat operations, post-conflict operations, and contingency operations. http://frwebgate.access.gpo.gov/cgi-bin/getdoc.cgi?_dbname=110_cong_bills&docid=f:h4986enr.txt.pdf

[56]William Long, "Joint Contingency Contracting: A Step Forward," Defense AT&L (May-June 2010). http://www.dau.mil/pubscats/Lists/ATL%20Database/Attachments/693/long_may-june10.pdf

[57]See https://acquire.dau.mil/Default.aspx

[58]"Ask a Professor", https://akss.dau.mil/askaprof-akss/default.aspx

[59]William Long, Joint *Contingency Contracting: A Step Forward*, Defense AT&L, May-June 2010. http://www.dau.mil/pubscats/Lists/ATL%20Database/Attachments/693/long_may-june10.pdf

[60]Maj Mark W. Lee, "The Commander's Emergency Response Program: Synergistic Results Through Training, *Army Sustainment*, May-June 2010. http://www.almc.army.mil/alog/issues/May-June10/synergy_thrutrain.html

Intentionally Blank

GLOSSARY
PART I—ABBREVIATIONS AND ACRONYMS

ADT	Agri-business Development Team
ANDS	Afghan National Development Strategy
ANSF	Afghan National Security Forces
AOR	area of responsibility
CALL	Center for Army Lessons Learned
CCJO	Capstone Concept for Joint Operations
CCO	contingency contracting officer
CERP	Commander's Emergency Response Program
CIA	Central Intelligence Agency
CIDNE	Combined Information Data Network Exchange
CJTF-HOA	Combined Joint Task Force- Horn of Africa
CLC	continuous learning course
CMO	civil military operations
CMOC	civil military operations center
COA	course of action
COI	community of interest
COIN	counterinsurgency
COM	Chief of Mission
CONOPS	concept of operations
COR	contracting officer's representative
CTF	Counter Threat Finance
DAU	Defense Acquisition University
DEA	Drug Enforcement Administration
DHHS	Department of Health and Human Services
dL	distributed learning
DOA	Department of Agriculture
DOD	Department of Defense
DODI	Department of Defense instruction
DOJ	Department of Justice
DOS	Department of State
DOTMLPF	doctrine, organization, training, materiel, leadership and education, personnel, and facilities
ESF	Economic Support Fund
EWG	Executive Working Group (deputies-level decision making body for USFOR-A Civilian–Military Campaign Plan)
FOB	forward operations base
FOO	field ordering officer
FPDS-NG	Federal Procurement Data System- Next Generation

GAO	Government Accountability Office
GIRoA	Government of the Islamic Republic of Afghanistan
GPC	Government Purchase Card (holders)
HQ	headquarters
ICAF	Interagency Conflict Assessment Framework
IFO	integrated financial operations
IGO	intergovernmental organization
ISAF	International Security Assistance Force
IT-P	Integrated Team-Provincial
IT-R	Integrated Team-Regional
IT-S	Integrated Team-Sub-regional
JCC-I/A	Joint Contracting Command-Iraq/Afghanistan (transitioning to USCENTCOM Contracting Command)
JFC	joint force commander
JOPP	joint operation planning process
JTF	joint task force
LGCD	local governance and community development program (embedded with PRT)
LOA	lines of activity
LOGCAP	Logistics Civilian Augmentation Program
MAAWS	Money as a Weapons System
MILCON	military construction
MMRD	Ministry of Rural Rehabilitation and Development (GIRoA)
MNC-I	Multi-National Corps-Iraq
MNF	multinational forces
MOE	measure of effectiveness
MOP	measure of performance
MPA	military personnel-army
MOU	memorandum of understanding
NATO	North Atlantic Treaty Organization
NDAA	National Defense Authorization Act
NDU	National Defense University
NGO	nongovernmental organization
NSP	National Solidarity Program
O&M	operations and maintenance
OSD	Office of the Secretary of Defense
PA	paying agent
PG	Principals' Group (USFOR-A decision-making group)

PPO	project purchasing officer
PRDC	provincial reconstruction & development committee
PRT	provincial reconstruction team
RM	resource management
S/CRS	State Coordinator for Reconstruction and Stabilization
SecDef	Secretary of Defense
SECSTATE	Secretary of State
SIGAR	Special Inspector General for Afghanistan Reconstruction
SIPRNET	Secret Internet Protocol Router Network
SOP	standard operating procedure
SPOT	Synchronized Predeployment and Operational Tracker
TADLP	The Army's Distributed Learning Program
TCAPF	Tactical Conflict Assessment Framework
TOPAS	Theater Operational Planning Assessment Service
TRADOC	US Army Training and Doctrine Command
TREAS	Department of the Treasury
UN	United Nations
UNAMA	United Nations Assistance Mission in Afghanistan
UNOCHA	United Nations Office for Coordination of Humanitarian Assistance
USAF	United States Air Force
USAID	United States Agency for International Development
USFOR-A	United States Forces-Afghanistan
USG	United States Government
USJFCOM	United States Joint Forces Command

Intentionally Blank

PART II—TERMS AND DEFINITIONS

adversary. A party acknowledged as potentially hostile to a friendly party and against which the use of force may be envisaged. (JP 1-02. SOURCE: JP 3-0)

assessment. 1. A continuous process that measures the overall effectiveness of employing joint force capabilities during military operations. 2. Determination of the progress toward accomplishing a task, creating an effect, or achieving an objective. 3. Analysis of the security, effectiveness, and potential of an existing or planned intelligence activity. 4. Judgment of the motives, qualifications, and characteristics of present or prospective employees or "agents." (JP 1-02. SOURCE: JP 3-0)

capability. The ability to execute a specified course of action. (A capability may or may not be accompanied by an intention.) (JP 1-02)

civil affairs. Designated Active and Reserve component forces and units organized, trained, and equipped specifically to conduct civil affairs activities and to support civil-military operations. Also called **CA**. (JP 1-02. SOURCE: JP 3-57)

civil affairs operations. Those military operations conducted by civil affairs forces that (1) enhance the relationship between military forces and civil authorities in localities where military forces are present; (2) require coordination with other interagency organizations, intergovernmental organizations, nongovernmental organizations, indigenous populations and institutions, and the private sector; and (3) involve application of functional specialty skills that normally are the responsibility of civil government to enhance the conduct of civil-military operations. Also called **CAO**. (JP 1-02: SOURCE: JP 3-57)

civil-military operations. The activities of a commander that establish, maintain, influence, or exploit relations between military forces, governmental and nongovernmental civilian organizations and authorities, and the civilian populace in a friendly, neutral, or hostile operational area in order to facilitate military operations, to consolidate and achieve operational US objectives. Civil-military operations may include performance by military forces of activities and functions normally the responsibility of the local, regional, or national government. These activities may occur prior to, during, or subsequent to other military actions. They may also occur, if directed, in the absence of other military operations. Civil military operations may be performed by designated civil affairs, by other military forces, or by a combination of civil affairs and other forces. Also called **CMO**. (JP 1-02. SOURCE: JP 3-57)

civil-military operations center. An organization normally comprised of civil affairs, established to plan and facilitate coordination of activities of the Armed Forces of the United States with indigenous populations and institutions, the private sector, intergovernmental organizations, nongovernmental organizations, multinational forces, and other governmental agencies in support of the joint force commander. Also called **CMOC**. See also **civil-military operations**. (JP 1-02. SOURCE: JP 3-57)

coalition. An ad hoc arrangement between two or more nations for common action. See also **multinational**. (JP 1-02. SOURCE: JP 5-0)

contracting officer. The Service member or Department of Defense civilian with the legal authority to enter into , administer, modify, and/or terminate contracts. (JP 1-02. SOURCE: JP 4-10)

counterinsurgency. Comprehensive civilian and military efforts taken to defeat an insurgency and to address any core grievances. Also called **COIN**. (JP 1-02. SOURCE: JP 3-24)

counterterrorism. Actions taken directly against terrorist networks and indirectly to influence and render global and regional environments inhospitable to terrorist networks. (JP 1-02. SOURCE: JP 3-26)

counter threat finance. Activities that attempt to deny, disrupt, destroy, or defeat financial systems and networks that negatively affect United States interests. Counter threat finance activities include, but are not limited to, countering narcotics trafficking, proliferation activities, weapons of mass destruction networks, trafficking in persons, weapons trafficking, precursor chemical smuggling, terrorist revenue and logistics, and other such activities that generate revenue through illicit networks. (No approved DOD definition, multiple USJFCOM sources)

country team. The senior, in-country, US coordinating and supervising body, headed by the chief of the US diplomatic mission, and composed of the senior member of each represented US department or agency, as desired by the chief of the US diplomatic mission. (JP 1-02. SOURCE: JP 3-07.4)

course of action. 1. Any sequence of activities that an individual or unit may follow. 2. A possible plan open to an individual or commander that would accomplish, or is related to the accomplishment of the mission. 3. The scheme adopted to accomplish a job or mission. 4. A line of conduct in an engagement. 5. A product of the Joint Operation Planning and Execution System concept development phase and the course of- action determination steps of the joint operation planning process. Also called **COA**. (JP 1-02. SOURCE: JP 5-0)

doctrine. Fundamental principles by which the military forces or elements thereof guide their actions in support of national objectives. It is authoritative but requires judgment in application. See also **joint doctrine**. (JP 1-02.)

end state. The set of required conditions that defines achievement of the commander's objectives. (JP 1-02. SOURCE: JP 3-0)

financial management. Financial management encompasses the two core functions of resource management and finance support. Also called **FM**. (JP 1-02. SOURCE: JP 1-06)

foreign assistance. Assistance to foreign nations ranging from the sale of military equipment to donations of food and medical supplies to aid survivors of natural and manmade disasters. US assistance takes three forms — development assistance, humanitarian assistance, and security assistance. (JP 1-02.)

host nation. A nation that receives the forces and/or supplies of allied nations, coalition partners, and/or NATO organizations to be located on, to operate in, or to transit through its territory. Also called **HN**. (JP 1-02. SOURCE: JP 3-57)

integrated financial operations (IFO). The integration, synchronization, prioritization and targeting of fiscal resources and capabilities across US agencies, multinational partners, and non-governmental organizations against an enemy and in support of the population, combined with minimizing the possibility that such resources/capabilities will be diverted or inadvertently misused to support an enemy's financial networks. (This term is used only in the context of this handbook.)

integration. The arrangement of military forces and their actions to create a force that operates by engaging as a whole. (JP 1-02. SOURCE: JP 1)

interagency coordination. Within the context of Department of Defense involvement, the coordination that occurs between elements of Department of Defense, and engaged US Government agencies for the purpose of achieving an objective. (JP 1-02. SOURCE: JP 3-0)

intergovernmental organization. An organization created by a formal agreement (e.g. a treaty) between two or more governments. It may be established on a global, regional, or functional basis for wide-ranging or narrowly defined purposes. Formed to protect and promote national interests shared by member states. Examples include the United Nations, North Atlantic Treaty Organization, and the African Union. Also called **IGO**. (JP 1-02. SOURCE: JP 3-08)

irregular warfare. A violent struggle among state and non-state actors for legitimacy and influence over the relevant population(s). Irregular warfare favors indirect and asymmetric approaches, although it may employ the full range of military and other capacities, in order to erode an adversary's power, influence, and will. Also called **IW**. (JP 1-02. SOURCE: JP 1-0)

insurgency. The organized use of subversion and violence by a group or movement that seeks to overthrow or force the change of a governing authority. Insurgency can also refer to the group itself. (JP 1-02. SOURCE: JP 3-24)

joint doctrine. Fundamental principles that guide the employment of US military forces in coordinated action toward a common objective. Joint doctrine contained in joint publications also includes terms, tactics, techniques, and procedures. It is authoritative but requires judgment in application. See also **doctrine**. (JP 1-02. SOURCE: CJCSI 5120.02)

joint force commander. A general term applied to a combatant commander, sub-unified commander, or joint task force commander authorized to exercise combatant command (command authority) or operational control over a joint force. Also called **JFC**. (JP 1-02.)

joint operation planning. Planning activities associated with joint military operations by combatant commanders and their subordinate joint force commanders in response to contingencies and crises. Joint operation planning includes planning for the mobilization, deployment, employment, sustainment, redeployment, and demobilization of joint forces. See also **joint operation planning process**. (JP 1-02. SOURCE: JP 5-0)

joint operation planning process. An orderly, analytical process that consists of a logical set of steps to analyze a mission; develop, analyze, and compare alternative courses of action against criteria of success and each other; select the best course of action; and produce a joint operation plan or order. Also called **JOPP**. See also **joint operation planning**. (JP 1-02. SOURCE: JP 5-0)

joint task force. A joint force that is constituted and so designated by the Secretary of Defense, a combatant commander, a sub-unified commander, or an existing joint task force commander. Also called **JTF**. (JP 1-02. SOURCE: JP 1)

lead agency. Designated among US Government agencies to coordinate the interagency oversight of the day-to-day conduct of an ongoing operation. The lead agency is to chair the interagency working group established to coordinate policy related to a particular operation. The lead agency determines the agenda, ensures cohesion among the agencies and is responsible for implementing decisions. (JP 1-02. SOURCE: JP 3-08)

materiel. All items (including ships, tanks, self-propelled weapons, aircraft, etc., and related spares, repair parts, and support equipment, but excluding real property, installations, and utilities) necessary to equip, operate, maintain, and support military activities without distinction as to its application for administrative or combat purposes. (JP 1-02. SOURCE: JP 4-0)

measure of effectiveness. A criterion used to assess changes in system behavior, capability, or operational environment that is tied to measuring the attainment of an end state, achievement of an objective, or creation of an effect. Also called **MOE**. (JP 1-02. SOURCE: JP 3-0)

measure of performance. A criterion used to assess friendly actions that is tied to measuring task accomplishment. Also called **MOP**. (JP 1-02. SOURCE: JP 3-0)

multinational. Between two or more forces or agencies of two or more nations or coalition partners. See also **alliance**; **coalition**. (JP 1-02. SOURCE: JP 5-0)

nongovernmental organization. A private, self-governing, not-for-profit organization dedicated to alleviating human suffering; and/or promoting education, health care, economic development, environmental protection, human rights, and conflict resolution;

and/or encouraging the establishment of democratic institutions and civil society. Also called **NGO**. (JP 1-02. SOURCE: JP 3-08)

operational area. An overarching term encompassing more descriptive terms for geographic areas in which military operations are conducted. Operational areas include, but are not limited to, such descriptors as area of responsibility, theater of war, theater of operations, joint operations area, amphibious objective area, joint special operations area, and area of operations. Also called **OA**. (JP 1-02. SOURCE: JP 3-0)

peacekeeping. Military operations undertaken with the consent of all major parties to a dispute, designed to monitor and facilitate implementation of an agreement (ceasefire, truce, or other such agreement) and support diplomatic efforts to reach a long-term political settlement. See also peace operations. (JP 1-02. SOURCE: JP 3-07.3)

peace operations. A broad term that encompasses peacekeeping operations and peace enforcement operations conducted in support of diplomatic efforts to establish and maintain peace. Also called **PO**. (JP 1-02. SOURCE: JP 3-07.3)

provincial reconstruction team. An interim interagency organization designed to improve stability in a given area by helping build the legitimacy and effectiveness of a host nation local or provincial government in providing security to its citizens and delivering essential government services. Also called **PRT**. (JP 1-02. SOURCE: JP 3-57)

resource management. A financial management function which includes providing advice and guidance to the commander, developing command resource requirements, identifying sources of funding, determining cost, acquiring funds, distributing and controlling funds, tracking costs and obligations, cost capturing and reimbursement procedures, providing accounting support, and establishing a management internal control process. Also called **RM**. See also **financial management**. (JP 1-02. SOURCE: JP 1-06)

security assistance. Group of programs authorized by the Foreign Assistance Act of 1961, as amended, and the Arms Export Control Act of 1976, as amended, or other related statutes by which the United States provides defense articles, military training, and other defense-related services by grant, loan, credit, or cash sales in furtherance of national policies and objectives. Also called **SA**. See also foreign assistance. (JP 1-02. SOURCE: JP 3-57)

stability operations. An overarching term encompassing various military missions, tasks, and activities conducted outside the United States in coordination with other instruments of national power to maintain or reestablish a safe and secure environment, provide essential governmental services, emergency infrastructure reconstruction, and humanitarian relief. (JP 1-02. SOURCE: JP 3-0)

stakeholders. Project stakeholders are those entities within or without an organization which: a) sponsor a project; or, b) have an interest, resource, or expected gain from the successful completion of a project. (Unified Action Handbook Series, Book Two: *Military Support to Essential Services and Critical Infrastructure*)

strategy. A prudent idea or set of ideas for employing the instruments of national power in a synchronized and integrated fashion to achieve theater, national, and/or multinational objectives. (JP 1-02. SOURCE: JP 3-0)

synchronization. 1. The arrangement of military actions in time, space, and purpose to produce maximum relative combat power at a decisive place and time. 2. In the intelligence context, application of intelligence sources and methods in concert with the operation plan to ensure intelligence requirements are answered in time to influence the decisions they support. (JP 1-02. SOURCE: JP 2-0)

targeting. The process of selecting and prioritizing targets and matching the appropriate response to them, considering operational requirements and capabilities. (JP 1-02. SOURCE: JP 3-0)

tactical conflict assessment and planning framework. To increase the effectiveness of stability operations, the U.S. Agency for International Development created the tactical conflict assessment and planning framework (TCAPF). The TCAPF was designed to assist commanders and their staffs identify the causes of instability, develop activities to diminish or mitigate them, and evaluate the effectiveness of the activities in fostering stability at the tactical level (provincial or local). The TCAPF should be used to create local stabilization plans and provide data for the Interagency Conflict Assessment Framework (ICAF), which has a strategic and operational-level (country or regional) focus. (Field Manual 3-07, Appendix D, Section D-34.)

unified action. The synchronization, coordination, and/or integration of the activities of governmental and nongovernmental entities with military operations to achieve unity of effort. (JP 1-02. SOURCE: JP 1)